INSIDE

YOUR MATCH ANNUAL 2020!

UK & IRELAND DREAM TEAM 40

ULTIMATE GUIDE TO... EURO 2020

Ahead of this summer's European Championship, MATCH gives you the lowdown on everything you need to look out for at the epic tournament!

1. TOURNO ON TOUR
6. SUPER SERGIO
7. FRENCH DEJA VU
2. MORE GOALS AND TEAMS
3. MEGA MASCOTS
8. RONALDO'S RECORDS
9. BATTLE FOR THE GOLDEN BOOT
4. WICKED WEMBLEY

EURO 2020 GUIDE 24

HEIR TO THE THRONE NO.5

JADON SANCHO!

THE NEXT... RAHEEM STERLING?

PLAYING STYLE!

BUNDESLIGA HEIRS!

THE KING!

THE HEIR!

HIS IMPACT!

WILL HE RULE?

STORY SO FAR...

TOP SKILLS!

JADON SANCHO 88

MESSI v RONALDO!

MATCH checks out why BARCELONA superstar LIONEL MESSI should be crowned the GOAT!

40+ GOAL MACHINE!

GETAFE GOAL!

LA LIGA LEGEND!

GUINNESS WORLD RECORD!

ARGENTINA ACE!

CLASICO KING!

BARCA BEAST!

GOLDEN SHOE STAR!

CL TOP-UP!

RONALDO v MESSI 76

THE GREATEST PREM TEAM EVER?

Back-to-back Premier League champions MAN CITY have been unstoppable over the past two seasons, and footy experts think they're the best side the Prem has ever seen! MATCH takes a closer look at their epic numbers and checks out the other contenders for the title!

82.13%

201

14

32

4

198

2

169

50

19

79

GREATNESS RATING 10/10

TURN OVER FOR MORE GREATEST PREM TEAM EVER CONTENDERS

MAN. CITY TREBLE WINNERS 14

FOOTBALL'S COMING HOME!

This summer, the home of football is hosting the final of the European Championship! With the EURO 2020 trophy heading to Wembley Stadium, will ENGLAND be there to lift it? MATCH reveals how football could be coming home...

AWESOME ATTACK!

England's attack is full of wicked talent! Raheem Sterling's link-up play with Harry Kane and Marcus Rashford blew Spain away in a 3-2 win in Seville in 2018 and, with more flair coming from midfield in Dele Alli, Jesse Lingard, Ross Barkley and Ruben Loftus-Cheek, The Three Lions have the attacking potential to destroy anybody in their path!

HURT & HUNGER!

England have suffered semi-final heartbreak in each of the last two summers - first they were beaten by Croatia at the 2018 World Cup, then they lost to Netherlands in the UEFA Nations League in 2019! The Three Lions will be desperate to bounce back from those extra-time defeats - and prove that they've learnt lessons from them!

SUPER STERLING!

Man. City are one of the best teams on the planet right now, and one of their biggest stars is Raheem Sterling! Since the World Cup, the forward has started bringing his red-hot club form to the national team, bagging six goals in seven UEFA Nations League and European qualifying games. He could be England's key man at Euro 2020!

PENALTY EXPERTS!

Before the 2018 World Cup, England had one of the worst penalty shootout records in history, with just one victory out of seven in major tournaments! It looks like Gareth Southgate's helped bury that hoodoo now, though – they overcame Colombia in Russia and beat Switzerland in last summer's Nations League, so if they face a shootout this summer, they'll be much more confident!

NEXT-GEN STARS!

In 2017, England's youth teams won loads of trophies, and the stars of those sides are ready to break through. Southgate has already played Trent Alexander-Arnold, Jadon Sancho and Callum Hudson-Odoi, and exciting young guns like James Maddison, Phil Foden, Rhian Brewster, Mason Mount and Ryan Sessegnon will be hoping to make his 23-man squad too!

LETHAL LIONESSES!

The women's team also made the country proud in 2019! With England hosting Euro 2021, we reveal five Lionesses we expect to totally tear it up between now and then...

LUCY BRONZE

After winning the Silver Ball at France 2019, the flying full-back will be hoping to add to her already bulging trophy cabinet at class European champions Lyon!

TONI DUGGAN

Duggan is an England forward ready for a new challenge - she left Barcelona Femeni last summer after two years there, only to join mega rivals Atletico!

ELLEN WHITE

After finishing as the joint top scorer at the World Cup, White is ready to take her game to the next level at new club Man. City - she'd love to win the league there!

NIKITA PARRIS

The speedy forward won the Women's Footballer Of The Year in 2019, before stepping out of her comfort zone to move to France and join Champo League holders Lyon!

JORDAN NOBBS

After missing the World Cup through injury, England vice-captain Nobbs is ready to rock for Arsenal and force her way back into Phil Neville's epic starting line-up!

FIVE FACES OF...
MESSI

Top Teenager
2004-07

Valdes

Oleguer | Puyol | Marquez | Van Bronckhorst

Xavi

Iniesta | Deco

MESSI | Eto'o | Ronaldinho

Messi burst onto the scene as one of the most exciting wonderkids on the planet! He was only 16 when he made his debut, but it didn't take him long to become a regular. The youngster was a real game-changer off the bench and back-up to first-choice right winger Ludovic Giuly. But, by the time he'd reached his 20s, he was undroppable!

Wicked Winger
2007-09

Valdes

Zambrotta | Puyol | Milito | Abidal

Toure

Xavi | Iniesta

MESSI | Eto'o | Henry

Once Ronaldinho had moved on, Messi took over as Barcelona's star man. Along with Xavi and Iniesta, he created loads of chances for Eto'o and Henry, as well as bagging tons himself. In 2008-09 he won his first Champions League Golden Boot with nine goals, including one in the final, and beat Cristiano Ronaldo to the Ballon d'Or for the first time!

> LIONEL MESSI has spent his whole career ripping it up at BARCELONA! MATCH tracks the five phases of his journey – from teenage prodigy to total footy legend!

TOP 5...
DEADLY DUOS!

Before the 2019-20 season kicked off, Man. City's David Silva had provided 18 Prem assists for Sergio Aguero – can the duo beat the all-time record?

1 Frank Lampard to Didier Drogba
Chelsea
⚽ 24 assists

2 Darren Anderton to Teddy Sheringham
Tottenham
⚽ 20 assists

3 Steve McManaman to Robbie Fowler
Liverpool
⚽ 20 assists

4 David Silva to Sergio Aguero
Man. City
⚽ 18 assists

5 Robert Pires to Thierry Henry
Arsenal
⚽ 17 assists

False Nine
2009-13

	Valdes	
Dani Alves	Mascherano Pique	Abidal
	Busquets	
Xavi		Iniesta
Pedro	MESSI	Villa

Pep Guardiola pulled off a masterstroke by moving Messi into the centre, and that's when he became an unstoppable goalscorer! From his new position, he dropped into midfield for possession, dribbled through the opposition and got on the end of chances in the box. He scored 91 goals in 2012 alone, and won his fourth Ballon d'Or in a row!

Perfect Playmaker
2013-17

	Ter Stegen	
Dani Alves	Mascherano Pique	Alba
	Busquets	
Rakitic		Iniesta
MESSI	Suarez	Neymar

The arrival of Neymar and Luis Suarez gave Barcelona the deadliest attack in footy history, and changed Messi's position again. Suarez took over as the main centre-forward, giving Leo the freedom to play wherever he wanted! 2015-16 was the first time in six years that he wasn't Barça's top scorer, but he assisted loads for his team-mates!

Legendary Leader
2017-19

	Ter Stegen	
Roberto	Pique Lenglet	Alba
	Busquets	
De Jong		Arthur
MESSI	Suarez	Griezmann

Since the departure of Neymar, Messi's taken on more responsibility for Barço's attacks, while also replacing Iniesta as club captain – and he's really risen to the challenge! In the last three campaigns, the legendary number ten scored 150 goals in just 156 matches. We can't wait to see his partnership with Antoine Griezmann grow!

FORGOTTEN CLUBS!

MATCH looks back through the history books to some of footy's most famous lost clubs!

WANDERERS ⚽ 1859-87

Nicknamed The Rovers, Wanderers were one of English football's early giants! They won the first ever FA Cup, and lifted the famous trophy five times before finally going out of business in 1887. Only nine teams have still won more FA Cups than them!

FIORENTINA ⚽ 1926-2002

Goal king Gabriel Batistuta made the Italians one of the best teams in Europe in the '90s, before they went bankrupt in 2002. They reformed that same summer with a brand-new name – Florentia Viola – but won back the right to be called Fiorentina in 2003!

NEW YORK COSMOS ⚽ 1970-85

Way before Major League Soccer was making its mark in the United States, the American Galacticos were signing up legendary superstars like Pele and Franz Beckenbauer! They folded in 1985 with the American league, but were re-born in 2010!

WIMBLEDON ⚽ 1889-2004

The Crazy Gang caused one of the biggest upsets ever to win the 1988 FA Cup! In protest to their move to Milton Keynes, their fans founded AFC Wimbledon – and, in 2011, they became the first club formed in the 21st century to make it into the Football League!

DID YOU KNOW?

In 2018, Liverpool scored seven goals in just two games against Alisson when he was in goal for Roma. But, after The Reds signed the Brazil keeper, it took the rest of the Premier League 17 matches to score that many past him!

STRANGER THINGS!

Antoine Griezmann's suggestion that he and team-mate Samuel Umtiti should star in the new series of Stranger Things was meant to be a joke – but a newspaper mistook it for a genuine old pic of the pair from when they were kids. LOL!

QUICK QUIZ!
Can you name the eight teams that have never been relegated from the Premier League?

Turn over for answers!

6 IS THE MAGIC NUMBER!

In 2019, LIVERPOOL confirmed their status as England's most successful club in European footy by winning their sixth Champions League trophy! MATCH gives you the lowdown on each of The Reds' European Cup triumphs...

1

1977
LIVERPOOL 3-1 B. M'GLADBACH

After smashing Zurich 6-1 on aggregate in the semis, Liverpool beat German champions Borussia Monchengladbach in the final. It was their second European trophy in a row after the 1976 UEFA Cup, and made them only the second English team to win the European Cup!

2

1978
LIVERPOOL 1-0 CLUB BRUGGE

The holders beat Gladbach again, this time in the semi-finals, before facing Belgian champions Club Brugge at Wembley. Liverpool legend Kenny Dalglish scored the only goal of the game, with a beautiful chip over the on-rushing goalkeeper, to keep the trophy on Merseyside!

Premier 🦁 League

QUICK QUIZ ANSWERS!
These teams have never been relegated from the Prem! Did you guess all eight correctly?

Man. United 🔴	Tottenham 🐓
Arsenal 🔴	Everton 🔵
Chelsea 🔵	Bournemouth 🍒
Liverpool 🔴	Brighton 🔵

CELEBRATION OF THE YEAR!

Remember when Mario Balotelli celebrated scoring for Marseille by busting out his phone and then uploading a video to Instagram? What a joker!

INTER MIAMI

2020 is a massive year for MLS! Inter Miami, owned by England and Man. United legend David Beckham, are finally joining the league and they'll want to make a big impact! Gossips reckon Becks is lining up some huge names for his new squad - watch this space!

1981

LIVERPOOL 1-0 REAL MADRID

After first-round defeats in 1978-79 and 1979-80, The Reds were desperate to get their crown back. Legendary midfielders Terry McDermott and Graeme Souness shared the top scorer prize with six goals each, while this is also the last time Real Madrid lost a European Cup final. Wow!

3

1984

LIVERPOOL 1-1 ROMA
Liverpool won 4-2 on penalties

Victory in 1984 confirmed The Reds' status as one of the continent's dominant clubs - only Real Madrid had won more European Cups! They faced Roma in their home stadium in the final, and beat them 4-2 in a tense penalty shootout - famous for goalkeeper Bruce Grobbelaar's funny wobbly-legs antics!

4

2005

AC MILAN 3-3 LIVERPOOL
Liverpool won 3-2 on penalties

This is Liverpool's most dramatic CL victory! They avoided a group-stage exit thanks to Steven Gerrard's epic last-gasp strike against Olympiacos, beat Chelsea 1-0 in the semis with a goal that didn't cross the line, then came from 3-0 down at half-time in the final to beat AC Milan on penalties in Istanbul. And breathe...

5

2019

TOTTENHAM 0-2 LIVERPOOL

After heartbreak in the 2018 final, it was redemption for The Reds in 2019! Their semi-final comeback against Barcelona will go down as one of the greatest in CL history, while victory over Spurs in the final was Jurgen Klopp's first trophy for the club, having lost six finals in a row with both The Reds and Dortmund!

6

FOOTY RICH LI$T!

Finance experts *FORBES* revealed the richest football stars on the planet from their 2019 earnings! Check it out...

1	**LIONEL MESSI** Barcelona	**£99.8 million**
2	**CRISTIANO RONALDO** Juventus	**£85.6 million**
3	**NEYMAR** PSG	**£82.5 million**
4	**PAUL POGBA** Man. United	**£25.9 million**
5	**ANDRES INIESTA** Vissel Kobe	**£25.5 million**
6	**ALEXIS SANCHEZ** Inter	**£24.2 million**
7	**KYLIAN MBAPPE** PSG	**£24 million**
8	**MESUT OZIL** Arsenal	**£23.7 million**
9	**OSCAR** Shanghai SIPG	**£22.8 million**
10	**ANTOINE GRIEZMANN** Barcelona	**£21.8 million**

STADIUM WATCH!

Check out some of the mind-blowing new stadiums just around the corner!

SAN SIRO INTER & AC MILAN

Inter and AC Milan's famous shared stadium is getting torn down and replaced soon!

NOU CAMP BARCELONA

Work to increase the capacity and add a long-awaited roof to Barça's ground starts in 2020!

BRAMLEY-MOORE DOCK STADIUM, EVERTON

The Toffees are hoping to move out of Goodison Park in 2023 to a new 52,000-seater stadium!

STADIO DELLA ROMA ROMA

Roma currently share the Stadio Olimpico with Lazio, but from 2022 they're hoping to play in this bad boy!

SELHURST PARK CRYSTAL PALACE

The Eagles have one of the noisiest Prem grounds - and it'll be even noisier with an extra 6,000 fans!

1 FA EURO 20

2020 EUROPEAN CHAMPIONSHIP!

The European Championship brightens up any summer! Euro 2016 was wicked with England, Wales, Northern Ireland and Republic Of Ireland all qualifying, and we're hoping for more of the same in 2020. There's loads to be excited about – check out our ultimate guide to the tourno on page 24!

2

COPA AMERICA!

If you missed the 2019 Copa America, don't panic – there's another one just around the corner! South America's finest are all going head-to-head once again this summer, with Colombia and Argentina co-hosting it. It all kicks off at the same time as the Euros, so there will basically be footy on 24/7!

3

WCL BATTLE!

There's one dominant team in Europe when it comes to women's footy. French giants Lyon are chasing their fifth Champo League title in a row, and the battle to wrestle the trophy away from them is gonna be as tough as ever – especially with Lionesses' Lucy Bronze and Nikita Parris in their line-up!

5 REASONS WHY...
2020 WILL ROCK!

Check out all the epic footy action that MATCH is looking forward to in the year ahead!

4

THE PREMIER LEAGUE RULES!

2019 proved that Premier League clubs are the top dogs in European football right now, with all-English clashes in both the Champions League and Europa League finals. Spanish clubs hold the record for most victories in both competitions, but the gap is closing, and it could get even narrower in 2020! Watch out...

MIND-BLOWING TITLE RACES!

Man. City and Liverpool produced an amazing title race in 2018-19, and we're hoping for a repeat this season! It could be close in Europe too – Atletico and Real Madrid's new-look XIs could put serious pressure on Barcelona, while Bayern Munich and Borussia Dortmund strengthened their sides and should provide another epic title shootout in Germany!

5

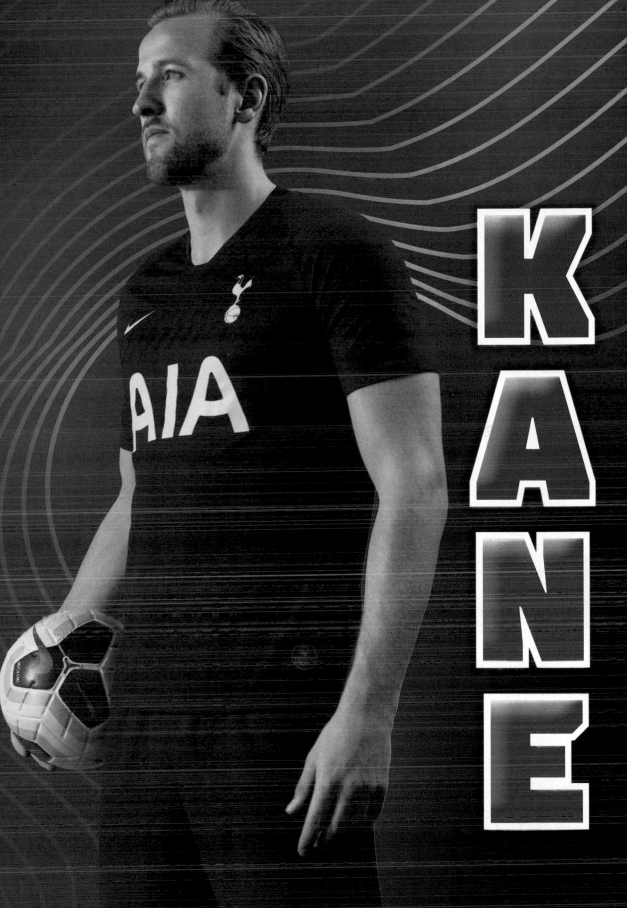

Fab Fact

Harry Kane loves NFL and says he wants to become a 'kicker' once he retires from footy!

Boots

Nike PhantomVNM

Stat Attack

He's scored over 20 goals in all comps in each of his last five seasons for Spurs!

Transfer Value

£150 million

KANE

JOAO FELIX

THE NEXT... CRISTIANO RONALDO?

THE KING...

The king of Portuguese footy needs no introduction! CR7 has been one of the best players on the planet for over a decade now, and Portugal captain for just as long. Not only is he their all-time top scorer, he's scored more international goals than any other European player ever and skippered his country to their first two trophies! Now that's what you call a LEGEND!

THE HEIR...

Full name: *Joao Felix Sequeira*
D.O.B: *10/11/1999*
Club: *Atletico Madrid*
Country: *Portugal*
Position: *Forward*
Boots: *adidas Copa 19+*

STORY SO FAR...

Felix and Ronaldo both started their pro careers in Lisbon, but with fiercely different clubs. While Cristiano made his debut for Sporting, the wonderkid started out at their fierce rivals Benfica, and quickly caught the eye of Europe's biggest clubs by scoring 20 goals in his first full season! In 2019, Atletico Madrid splashed out £113 million to make him the most expensive star in Portuguese history – and the third in world football!

HIS IMPACT!

Felix's transfer to Atletico is similar to CR7's move to Man. United back in 2003. Like the king, the wonderkid has joined one of the toughest leagues in Europe for a record fee and as a replacement for an outgoing legend. Cristiano was bought after the departure of David Beckham and given his old number seven shirt, just as Felix replaced Antoine Griezmann and was handed Atleti's No.7!

PLAYING STYLE!

Like Ronaldo, Felix began as a winger and bagged his first goal for Benfica by cutting in from the left and heading in a cross. But his best position is through the middle – he's got quick feet and quality technique to look after the ball in tight spaces, plus a sick eye for a pass and deadly finishing when he gets the chance. He doesn't have CR7's physicality, but he'll get stronger!

WILL HE RULE?

At Felix's age, Ronaldo was a raw talent with flashes of brilliance, but it took him a while to become the devastating goal machine that we know now. The young gun still has loads of time to develop and he'll be able to learn directly off Cristiano – they'll be spearheading the European champions' attack for the next few years as part of one of the deadliest strikeforces in international football!

TOP SKILLS!

SPEED	80
DRIBBLING	85
CREATIVITY	87
FINISHING	83
MOVEMENT	79

THE GREATEST

Back-to-back Premier League champions MAN. CITY have been unstoppable over the past two seasons, and footy experts think they're the best side the Prem has ever seen! MATCH takes a closer look at their epic numbers and checks out the other contenders for the crown...

14

Over the past two seasons, City have gone on the two best winning runs in Prem history! They sealed the 2018-19 title with an incredible streak of 14 victories, having won 18 in a row the season before!

198

They've bagged the most points as well! Their haul of 98 in 2018-19 was only bettered by their amazing 100-point season in 2017-18!

32

They've got 32 victories in each of the last two seasons – a Premier League record for a single campaign!

4

City have now won four Premier League titles – only rivals Man. United on 13 and Chelsea with five have won it on more occasions!

2

Prem title glory in 2019 made City the first side to retain the Premier League trophy since Man. United did it in 2008-09!

PREM TEAM EVER?

82.13%

In March 2018, the pass-masters set two PL records, first by completing over 900 passes against Chelsea then retaining 82.13% possession against Everton. Wowzers!

In the last two seasons they've busted 201 Prem nets, including a record 106 goals in 2017-18!

201

They also hold the record for the best ever goal difference in a Premier League season, with +79 in 2017-18!

79

GREATNESS RATING

10/10

169

City scored more goals in all comps in 2018-19 than any English top-flight team ever have in a single season, beating their previous record of 156 in 2013-14!

Pep Guardiola's team rule on the road too! In 2017-18, City set a Premier League record by winning 16 away matches and bagging 50 points!

50

19

In 2017-18, they finished 19 points ahead of rivals Man. United - the biggest title-winning margin in Premier League history!

TURN OVER FOR MORE GREATEST PREM TEAM EVER CONTENDERS!

THE RIVALS!

GREATNESS RATING 8/10

GREATNESS RATING 7/10

CHELSEA 2016-17

It took Pep Guardiola a year to settle into Prem life, but not Antonio Conte. The Chelsea boss took the league by storm when he arrived - his new 3-4-3 system outfoxed every other gaffer as The Blues cruised to the title with a record 30 wins, but City have since beaten that record!

LIVERPOOL 2017-19

Jurgen Klopp's side picked up an unwanted record in 2018-19, becoming the best team NOT to win the title! Their points tally of 97 has only been beaten twice but, unfortunately for them, both of those were Man. City in the last two seasons. The Reds need to win the 2019-20 title to become the best!

GREATNESS RATING 6/10

GREATNESS RATING 6/10

MAN. CITY 2011-14

City's first title-winning team can definitely claim the greatest Premier League moment. Sergio Aguero's dramatic title-winning goal in the dying seconds of the 2011-12 season against QPR will never be forgotten! But, unlike the current team, they had to wait two years to get their hands on the Prem trophy again!

CHELSEA 2009-10

In Carlo Ancelotti's first season as Chelsea gaffer, The Blues pipped Man. United to the title by a single point, ending The Red Devils' run of three titles in a row! Didier Drogba and Frank Lampard helped The Blues score 103 goals - a record that City have since gone on to break!

MAN. UNITED 2006-09

This team had everything, with Rio Ferdinand and Nemanja Vidic dominating the defence, Paul Scholes running the midfield and a devastating front three of Cristiano Ronaldo, Wayne Rooney and Carlos Tevez! They won three titles in a row and also reached two Champo League finals, so Pep's City have some catching up to do!

GREATNESS RATING 8/10

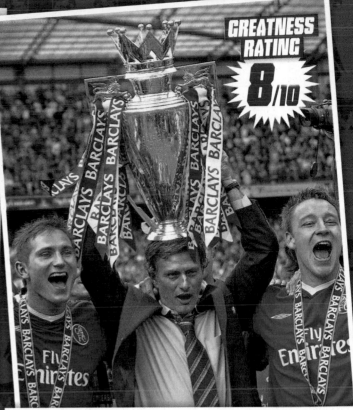

CHELSEA 2004-06

Jose Mourinho is known for defensive footy, and his first Chelsea team still holds the record for most clean sheets (24) and fewest goals conceded (15) in a single PL season! But they were also a devastating counter-attacking team, and the back-to-back Prem winners would be a wicked match for the current City team!

GREATNESS RATING 8/10

ARSENAL 2003-04

The first and only undefeated Prem champions were rock solid at the back and inspired by the brilliance of Thierry Henry in attack! 'The Invincibles' will be remembered as one of the greatest teams in the history of the Premier League, although they did draw 12 matches – City have drawn half as many in the last two seasons combined!

GREATNESS RATING 9/10

MAN. UNITED 1998-99

In 1999, United became the first and only team to win the treble – the Prem, Champions League and FA Cup in the same season! The epic achievement was made even more special because the team was packed with homegrown talent like David Beckham, Ryan Giggs, Paul Scholes and Gary Neville. Sick!

GREATNESS RATING 8/10

BIG MATCH! QUIZ

PREMIER LEAGUE SPECIAL

FLASHBACK!

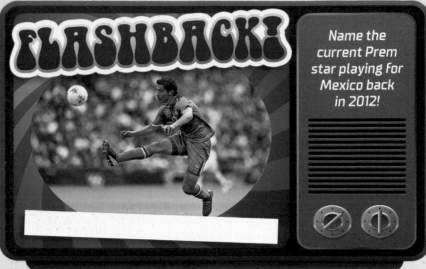

Name the current Prem star playing for Mexico back in 2012!

5 QUESTIONS ON...

ASTON VILLA

1 What year were Aston Villa founded – 1745, 1874, 1902, 1916 or 1953?

2 They're known as The Villans, but what's another of their awesome nicknames – The Lions, The Tigers, The Crows, The Wasps or The Leopards?

3 Which of these Prem legends never played for Aston Villa – James Milner, Gary Cahill, Gabby Agbonlahor, Robert Huth, Steven Davis or Gareth Barry?

4 What is Villa's best ever finish in the Premier League era – second, third, fourth, sixth, seventh or ninth?

5 True or False? Manager Dean Smith was a boyhood fan of The Villans!

CLOSE-UP!

Which Prem superstars have we zoomed in on?

1.

2.

3.

4.

CAMERA SHY!

Name the ballers hiding from the MATCH snapper in these pics from 2018-19!

PREM CHALLENGE

Match these top-quality grounds to the clubs that play there!

Bramall Lane	St. Mary's	The Amex	Carrow Road
1	2	3	4

A	B	C	D
Brighton	Norwich	Sheffield United	Southampton

FREAKY FACES!

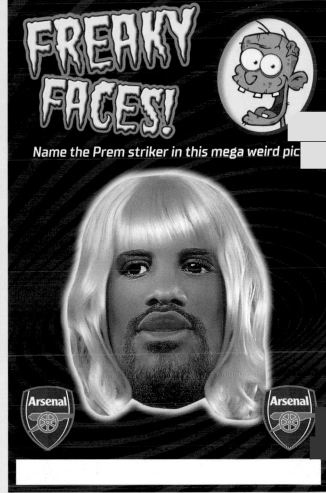

Name the Prem striker in this mega weird pic

Arsenal   Arsenal

Crystal Palace

Newcastle

SUPER SKIPPERS!

Can you name these Prem teams' club captains?

Tottenham

West Ham

Prem Heroes!

Which teams do these superstars play for?

1. Callum Wilson

2. Gerard Deulofeu

3. Davinson Sanchez

4. Ben Mee

5. Scott McTominay

6. Demarai Gray

7. Lucas Torreira

8. Oleksandr Zinchenko

CRAZY KIT!

Which side wore this crazy home kit from 1992 to 1994?

ANSWERS ON PAGE 94

CROSSWORD CRUNCH!

Use these clues to fill in MATCH's Premier League footy crossword!

ACROSS

3. Mega boot brand that Spurs striker Harry Kane wears! (4)

5. Main colour of West Ham's away kit for 2019-20! (5)

8. First name of Man. United's rock-solid defender, Maguire! (5)

9. Newcastle mascots Monty and Maggie are this type of bird! (6)

10. Number of Premier League titles that Arsenal have won! (5)

12. Premier League team that Lloyd Kelly plays for! (11)

14. Team that Luis Suarez left Liverpool to join in 2014! (9)

16. Country that epic gaffer Mauricio Pochettino is from! (9)

19. The Premier League top goalscorer in 2014-15! (6, 6)

21. First name of Leicester and Denmark shot-stopper Kasper Schmeichel's legendary dad! (5)

22. Huge sports brand that designed Southampton's mega cool 2019-20 strips! (5, 6)

23. Superstar with the most Prem assists in 2018-19! (4, 6)

DOWN

1. Winners of the 2016-17 Premier League title! (6)

2. Shirt number Dele Alli wears for Tottenham! (6)

3. Month that epic trickster Wilfried Zaha was born! (8)

4. Month Daniel James signed for Man. United in 2019! (4)

6. Wicked nickname of the club that plays at Turf Moor! (3, 7)

7. Number of Prem titles Cristiano Ronaldo won! (5)

11. Shirt number that Jamie Vardy wears for Leicester! (4)

13. Name of Man. United's jaw-dropping stadium! (3, 8)

15. Team that Everton signed keeper Jonas Lossl from! (12)

17. Position that Prem legend David James played! (10)

18. Country that Pierre-Emerick Aubameyang plays for! (5)

20. Former legendary 6ft 7in striker, Peter _ _ _ _ _ _ ! (6)

21. Boot brand that top-class playmaker David Silva wears! (4)

ANSWERS ON PAGE 94

MATCH!
THE BEST FOOTBALL MAGAZINE!

Fab Fact

Lingard came through Man. United's youth academy with good mate Paul Pogba!

Boots

adidas Nemeziz

Stat Attack

He's scored goals at Wembley in FA Cup and League Cup final wins for The Red Devils!

Transfer Value

£60 million

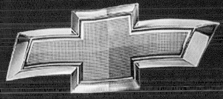

LINGARD

SNAPPED!
BEST OF 2019!

The chicken dance!

Richarlison and Gabriel Jesus went on the hunt for tasty pellets!

PUK PUK!

PUKAAK!

Sherbet surprise!

Anthony Knockaert ate too many sherbet lemons!

MY TONGUE BURNS!

IT'S STINGING MY EYES!

Shampoo shocker!

Cristiano forgot to wash away the shampoo after his shower...

HMM... LOOKS LIKE IT'S 4-3-3!

Mission impossible!

Ellen White was sent to spy on The Lionesses' World Cup opponents!

Blues bumps!

Gary Cahill didn't enjoy his Chelsea bumps one bit!

PUT ME DOWN NOW!

ULTIMATE GUIDE TO...
EURO 2020

Ahead of this summer's European Championship, MATCH gives you the lowdown on everything you need to look out for at the epic tournament!

1 TOURNO ON TOUR

For the first time in the Euros' history, there's no host country! Instead, the games will be played at 12 different cities across Europe to celebrate the tournament's 60th birthday. Check out each of the grounds on the next page!

2 MORE GOALS AND TEAMS

The 2016 tournament was the highest-scoring in Euros history, after 24 teams took part for the first time. That epic record of 108 could be broken in 2020, while more teams could also make their Euros debuts, with March's play-offs set to include some of the lower-ranked countries from the Nations League!

3 MEGA MASCOTS

There are three main mascots at next summer's comp, with wicked freestylers Liv Cooke and Tobias Becs joined by Skillzy! We're hoping to see some wicked tricks from the trio, after they put on an awesome show during their reveal last March!

4 WICKED WEMBLEY

Spoiler alert - the semi-finals and final will be played at England's national stadium! The Three Lions are dreaming of lifting the trophy at their home ground, in a clash that will set a new record attendance for a Euros final!

5 PERFECT PORTUGAL

Holders Portugal will have something to say about that, though! They've got even better since winning Euro 2016 - as they proved by bagging last summer's UEFA Nations League - and with rising stars like Bernardo Silva and Joao Felix, they're a force to be reckoned with!

6 SUPER SERGIO

Legendary Spain captain Sergio Ramos is chasing some epic Euros records. If the defender guides his team to the final, he'll be the first ever player to reach that stage three times, and could also be the first star to win the class competition three times!

7 FRENCH DEJA VU

When France won the World Cup in 1998, Les Bleus followed it up by winning the Euros two years later at Euro 2000 – and now history could repeat itself! The world champions have got one of the best squads in the world with Paul Pogba, N'Golo Kante, Kylian Mbappe and Antoine Griezmann, and they'll be one of the major favourites this summer!

8 RONALDO'S RECORDS

We don't need to tell you who the main man will be in Portugal's bid for the trophy! Cristiano Ronaldo has already played more games at the Euros than anyone else, but he could also become the outright all-time top scorer and the first man to play at five different tournaments!

9 BATTLE FOR THE GOLDEN BOOT

Griezmann was the top scorer in 2016, but he'll have loads of rivals for the 2020 award! France team-mate Mbappe could make a big statement, Harry Kane bagged the award at the World Cup, while joint all-time Euros top scorer Ronaldo is also chasing the prize!

10 GERMAN FIGHTBACK

Nobody's won more matches or tournaments in Euros history than Germany, but they've got a huge point to prove after crashing out in the group stage at World Cup 2018. Nobody will want to come up against them, because they'll be desperate to impress!

NOW TURN OVER FOR OUR EURO 2020 STADIUM GUIDE!

EURO 2020...
STADIUM GUIDE

Check out the grounds all around Europe that will be hosting this summer's Euros!

OLYMPIC STADIUM

Baku, Azerbaijan
Capacity: 68,700

Arsenal and Chelsea will remember Baku from the 2019 Europa League final. Most fans will be hoping to avoid the trip to Azerbaijan if their team manages to reach the quarters – it's miles away!

KRESTOVSKY STADIUM

Saint Petersburg, Russia ★ Capacity: 64,468

Zenit's wicked stadium was built ahead of the 2017 Confederations Cup, and hosted loads of matches at the 2018 World Cup, including France v Belgium in the semis and England's third-place play-off loss!

PUSKAS ARENA

Budapest, Hungary
Capacity: 67,889

Hungary's national stadium is named after their legendary forward Ferenc Puskas, and it's been totally rebuilt in the last couple of years. After re-opening in 2019, it'll be the newest ground in the comp!

PARKEN STADIUM

Copenhagen, Denmark
Capacity: 38,065

FC Copenhagen's ground might be the smallest at the tournament but, with nearly 40,000 fans crammed in, it should be one of the noisiest – especially if the retractable roof has to be closed up!

HAMPDEN PARK

Glasgow, Scotland
Capacity: 51,866

Scotland supporters have been waiting 22 years for their team to reach a major tournament, but now a Euros is coming to them! The national stadium will be the oldest ground at the 2020 European Championship!

SAN MAMES

Bilbao, Spain
Capacity: 53,289

The Bernabeu and Nou Camp might be Spain's most famous grounds, but when it comes to atmosphere not many can match Bilbao's San Mames! The stadium was rebuilt in 2013 – 100 years after the original!

ALLIANZ ARENA

Munich, Germany
Capacity: 70,000

Germany was spoilt for choice when picking their stadium to host a quarter-final match, but we think they made the right decision by picking Bayern Munich's ground. Not only is it massive, it looks spectacular!

WEMBLEY STADIUM

London, England
Capacity: 90,000

The home of English football is the perfect place for major matches, and that's why it's hosting both the semi-finals and the final! Since it's been rebuilt, two Champions League finals have been played at Wembley, but this will be the first international final there since the 2012 Olympics!

AVIVA STADIUM

Dublin, Republic Of Ireland ★ Capacity: 51,700

Ireland's famous old Landsdowne Road stadium was replaced by the super futuristic Aviva in 2010. It hosts rugby matches just as often as it does football, but this summer footy will definitely be boss!

JOHAN CRUYFF ARENA

Amsterdam, Netherlands ★ Capacity: 54,990

Ajax and Netherlands' awesome stadium has experience when it comes to hosting Euro matches, because it was one of the main grounds at Euro 2000 – hosted by the Netherlands and Belgium!

ARENA NATIONALA

Bucharest, Romania
Capacity: 55,634

You might not have seen Romania's national stadium in use too often, but we reckon it's one of the coolest-looking in Europe! The huge screen hanging over the top of the pitch will look incredible!

STADIO OLIMPICO

Rome, Italy
Capacity: 70,634

Italy was another country with loads of wicked stadiums to nominate for the Euros, but the ground shared by Lazio, Roma and the national team is a good choice. It hosted the World Cup final in 1990!

AGUERO

MODRIC

CARROLL

FALCAO

MARCELO

KUN STARTED THE 'GOING GREY' TREND!

I USED A WHOLE TUB OF WAX!

SALAH

BALE

GUENDOUZI

OTAMENDI

NEYMAR

WHO SAID MAN BUNS WERE 'SO 2018'?

MY BLOND LOCKS ROCK!

2019'S... CRAZIEST HAIRSTYLES!

Check out some of the weird and wonderful footy haircuts from 2019!

BELLERIN

CHOUDHURY

CAVANI

MANE

AUBAMEYANG

BEST 'FRO IN THE PREM!

MY HAIR DRYER BROKE!

MARTINEZ

GERVINHO

POGBA

HERNANDEZ

BALOTELLI

YOU CAN USE ME AS A TORCH!

GRIEZMANN

HAMSIK

VIDAL

LUIZ

SANCHES

MY MOHAWK DEFO BEATS VIDAL'S!

MATTHIJS DE LIGT!

THE NEXT... VIRGIL VAN DIJK?

THE KING...

Quite simply, Virgil van Dijk is the best centre-back in the world right now. Since arriving at Anfield in January 2018, he's not just transformed Liverpool's defence into one of the toughest in Europe, but raised standards throughout the rest of the squad too! In 2019, he became the first defender since 2005 to win the PFA Player Of The Year award and then inspired The Reds to glory in the Champions League!

THE HEIR...

Full name: *Matthijs de Ligt*

D.O.B: *12/08/1999*

Club: *Juventus*

Country: *Netherlands*

Position: *Centre-back*

Boots: *adidas X 18.1*

STORY SO FAR...

It's hard to believe, but van Dijk suffered loads of rejection at the start of his career. He was released on a free by Willem II and then sold by Groningen, but De Ligt is the total opposite. The wonderkid was an Ajax regular, club captain and Dutch international before he'd even turned 18! After skippering the club to a league and cup double, plus the Champions League semi-finals, he was sold to Juventus for a club-record £67.5 million!

PLAYING STYLE!

The Dutch duo are a top-quality partnership because they can do absolutely everything! They read the game brilliantly and take up perfect positions and, if they do ever get caught out, they're quick enough to make up for it. On top of that, they can pass the ball out of defence like midfielders and attack at corners like strikers! Although VVD wears the captain's armband for Netherlands, his young partner is just as much of a leader!

HIS IMPACT!

Van Dijk's had a massive impact at Liverpool, and not just through being a brilliant player. The centre-back proved that you don't have to be an attacker to inspire your team-mates and raise performances, and De Ligt did the same at Ajax. After he burst onto the scene, the club reached their first major European final for over two decades, won their first domestic double in 17 years and stunned the whole of Europe in the Champions League!

WILL HE RULE?

What De Ligt achieved at Ajax has already made him a footy megastar but, unlike his Netherlands team-mate, the young defender missed out on the top prize in 2019 with Van Dijk lifting the Champions League trophy for Liverpool. After joining Cristiano Ronaldo at Juventus, the wonderkid has a great chance of adding to his trophy collection – and proving that he's the true king of Dutch defenders!

TOP SKILLS!

STRENGTH		90
SPEED		75
TACKLING		85
POSITIONING		85
PASSING		79

SERIE A HEIRS!

Check out more wonderkids totally ripping it up in Italy...

GIANLUIGI DONNARUMMA

The next... Gianluigi Buffon?

Italy always seems to have a great goalkeeper between the sticks, and AC Milan's Donnarumma is definitely fit to fill Buffon's gloves for years to come!

NICOLO ZANIOLO

The next... Francesco Totti?

Roma fans are seriously excited about Zaniolo! The attacker, who made his Italy debut in March 2019, is being tipped to be the capital club's next Totti!

SANDRO TONALI

The next... Andrea Pirlo?

A deep-lying playmaker with long hair and a brilliant passing range who's making his name at Brescia – the similarities are clear!

LUCAS PAQUETA

The next... Kaka?

Like Kaka, Paqueta left Brazil to join AC Milan, and he glides through tackles just like the legendary midfielder!

FABIAN

The next... Xavi?

The Napoli midfielder was named best player at the 2019 Euro U21s, and he's gonna totally boss Spain's midfield!

MATCH! CHATS TO THE STARS!

Over the past year, we've chatted to absolutely tons of football superstars! Get a load of some of our favourite quotes that have featured in MATCH magazine...

LUKE SHAW

The Man. United star has taken on Ronaldo, Messi and Mbappe, so we were shocked when we found out who his toughest opponent was!

LUKE SAYS: "My toughest direct opponent has always been Victor Moses – I've always said that. He's so direct and strong, and when I first played against him I was quite young and inexperienced, so I always remember that being a really tough game!"

WILFRIED ZAHA

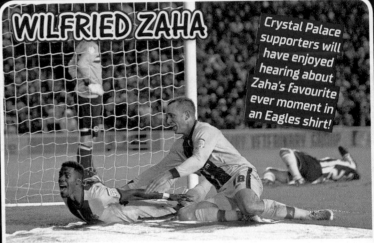

Crystal Palace supporters will have enjoyed hearing about Zaha's favourite ever moment in an Eagles shirt!

WILF SAYS: "My favourite moment is the goals I scored against Brighton in the play-offs. Not just for the rivalry, but the odds against us – Glenn Murray got injured so we were missing our main goalscorer. They were saying we'd lose because we had no-one to score, but I was the one who stepped up!"

HARRY WINKS

Tottenham and England central midfielder Winks got seriously star-struck when he met one of his fave players!

HARRY SAYS: "Going to watch Tottenham as a youngster, I just loved Jermain Defoe – he was my hero, so it was surreal to go away with England and play in the same team! I was star-struck when I met him, because I used to sing his name in my living room and had his name on the back of my shirt!"

JADON SANCHO

After the Dortmund wonderkid revealed his footy hero, it's obvious why he's got tons of tricks in his locker!

JADON SAYS: "Growing up, I used to watch Ronaldinho on YouTube. That was a big thing for me – I liked how he used to carry his team with his performances. He would try things that no-one else would – and that made me like him a lot!"

JAMES WARD-PROWSE

The Southampton and England free-kick king was feeling a little blue after his first ever pro goal!

JAMES SAYS: "My first goal was against Coventry in the FA Cup. I got into the box, Adam Lallana crossed the ball in and I managed to get a good contact on it. When I celebrated I pointed to the back of my shirt and stuck my tongue out – which was blue because I'd had a Powerade at half-time!"

HARRY MAGUIRE

The England defender's memories of Russia got MATCH wishing it was the summer of 2018 all over again!

HARRY SAYS: "We had an unbelievable summer – I'm really proud of the memories we created. I see clips and still get that buzz, but I still have something inside me which is disappointed too. It makes me feel a bit gutted that we had one foot in the final of a World Cup! It was really special and we want to do it again…"

JORDAN PICKFORD

MATCH was left a bit puzzled by the England and Everton goalkeeper's wacky superstition!

JORDAN SAYS: "I haven't asked the other Everton lads about their superstitions, but I have one myself - my shinpads have to be the right height. I'll wear them where they feel comfortable, but they must be the same height on both legs!"

TOM DAVIES

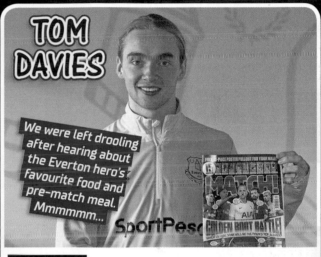

We were left drooling after hearing about the Everton hero's favourite food and pre-match meal. Mmmmmm…

TOM SAYS: "I love Chinese food! A friend of mine cooks it really well. I like most types of food really – I'll try most things. My typical matchday meal is toast with peanut butter and jam, and a cup of tea!

AARON CRESSWELL

The West Ham left-back wasn't too complimentary when we asked who his smartest team-mate was last season…

AARON SAYS: "Andy Carroll thinks he's clever, but he couldn't be further from it! We do quizzes at the back of the bus and he thinks he knows every answer, but we all just laugh. Robert Snodgrass will chirp up too, but he hasn't got a clue either!"

BIG MATCH! QUIZ

INTERNATIONALS SPECIAL

FOOTY AT THE FILMS!

Which Germany superstar has been given a major role in Toy Story 4?

5 QUESTIONS ON...
BELGIUM

1 What is the mega European nation's cool nickname – The Red Warriors, The Red Vikings or The Red Devils?

2 Which top-quality defender holds the record for most all-time caps – Toby Alderweireld, Vincent Kompany, Jan Vertonghen or Thomas Meunier?

3 Which forward has busted more nets for Belgium than anyone else – Eden Hazard or Romelu Lukaku?

4 True or False? They've never won the World Cup or European Championship!

5 Which international giants knocked them out of the 2018 World Cup in the semi-finals – France or Brazil?

CLOSE-UP!

Which international heroes have we zoomed in on?

1.

2.

3.

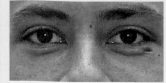
4.

SOCCER SCRABBLE

Which Three Lions goal machine's name is all jumbled up here?

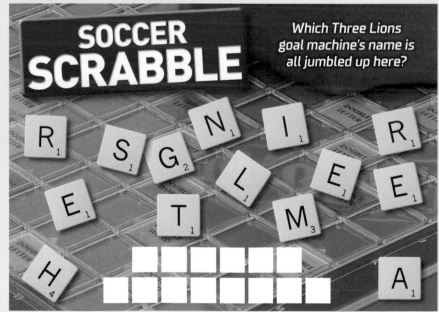

SPOT THE BALL!

Mark where you think the ball is in this cool International pic!

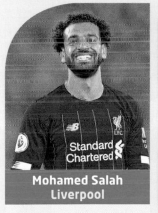

Mohamed Salah
Liverpool

Christian Pulisic
Chelsea

NAME THE COUNTRY!

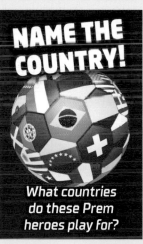

What countries do these Prem heroes play for?

Bernardo Silva
Man. City

Neil Taylor
Aston Villa

WHO AM I?

Can you work out the mystery star from the three clues below?

↘ I played over 25 times for my nation at youth level!

↘ I made my senior debut in 2017 against the Netherlands!

↘ I play as a central midfielder in my home country for champs Celtic!

MATCH! WINNER!

Name the Portugal star that scored their 2019 Nations League final winner v the Netherlands!

ANSWERS ON PAGE 94

Women's WC BRAIN-BUSTER!

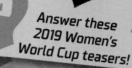

Answer these 2019 Women's World Cup teasers!

1. How many goals did France score against South Korea in the opener?

2. And in what stadium was the tournament opener played in – Parc des Princes or Stade de France?

3. How many times did Alex Morgan bust net in USA's 13-0 thrashing of Thailand?

4. Name the Brazilian who broke the record for all-time World Cup goals!

5. Who did England lose 2-1 to in the third-place play-off in Nice?

6. What was the score in the final between USA and Netherlands?

7. What was the name of the official mascot – Ettie, Betty or Leti?

8. How many red cards were there in total in the competition – three or four?

9. Name the lethal England striker that finished the tournament with six goals!

10. Which USA superstar was named the best player – Alex Morgan, Rose Lavelle or Megan Rapinoe?

1 ....
2 ....
3 ....
4 ....
5 ....
6 ....
7 ....
8 ....
9 ....
10 ....

ANSWERS ON PAGE 94

Fab Fact

Before joining Lyon back in 2017, Bronze played for Man. City, Liverpool, Everton and Sunderland!

Boots

Nike PhantomVNM

Stat Attack

Bronze was one of only two England stars at the 2019 World Cup with a Champo League winners' medal!

Transfer Value

£25 million

BRONZE

danialves

SPFC

Alves' favourite hashtag is #GoodCrazyMood – which is basically an excuse for him to post wacky pics and videos doing crazy things like singing, dancing, wearing his wife's high-heels and taking tons of LOL selfies with his cat!

+27m followers

iamzlatanibrahimovic

LA GALAXY

Zlatan's a proper character on and off the pitch, so obviously his Insta account is great value too! His captions are always funny as well – this one was, 'Mickey Mouse and Goofy!', although he normally calls himself 'God'!

+37m followers

MATCH reckons these are the footy superstars you need to be following on Instagram!

Stars to

---

paulpogba

MANCHESTER UNITED

Although Pogba's Insta sometimes feels like it should be your local barber's account with the amount of hair shots, he also posts throwback snaps of when he was growing up, holiday pics and funny photos at different adidas events!

+36m followers

kylewalker2

MANCHESTER CITY

Walks' account is well underrated! As well as jumping on silly trends, like uploading a pic of himself with an egg, he also posts screengrabs from his Twitter account – which normally feature banter with his City team-mates!

+1m followers

aubameyang97

Auba is mega cool, and the best thing about his Insta account is getting a glimpse of his incredible collection of wheels! He owns loads of supercars like a Ferrari, Lamborghini and Aston Martin! Can MATCH catch a ride?!

+8m followers

 neymarjr

Whether he's meeting other celebrities, showing off his latest custom-made Nike kicks or just fooling around in mad outfits, you can get a decent insight into the life of the most expensive player on the planet!

+124m followers

Follow!

 mosalah

Salah loves a selfie – plus pizza and fishing by the looks of these cool snaps! The Egyptian king shares loads of photos from his holidays, plus cool pics from training with his Liverpool team-mates and while on international duty!

+30m followers

 esmuellert

Muller's like the German version of Alexis Sanchez – he posts loads of snaps with his pets! As well as having dogs like Alexis, he's got a horse called Dave and another called Manuel – it was born the same day as Neuer!

+6m followers

UK & IRELAND DREAM TEAM!

MATCH wants to take a squad to EURO 2020 made up of players from the UK & Ireland, but we need YOU to pick the players! Send us your choices and you could win a top prize!

EURO 2020 DREAM TEAM
GOALKEEPERS!

JORDAN PICKFORD
ENGLAND
As well as having rockets on his boots to launch counter-attacks, Pickford's also a penalty expert – he was in goal for The Three Lions' first ever World Cup shootout win v Colombia in 2018, and is the only England GK in history to score a pen in a competitive game!

WAYNE HENNESSEY
WALES
If you're on the hunt for a keeper with bundles of international experience, Hennessey is definitely your man! He's won over 80 caps for The Dragons since making his debut back in 2007, and is in their top five for all-time appearances. He's also the tallest GK on our shortlist!

DAVID MARSHALL
SCOTLAND
Marshall made his international debut three years before Hennessey, but has over 50 fewer caps due to having to compete with Craig Gordon and Allan McGregor! The 34-year-old is back in favour ahead of Scott Bain, and still has the presence to shut out strikers!

DARREN RANDOLPH
REPUBLIC OF IRELAND
When your dad's an ex-basketball star, you're likely to have inherited a safe pair of hands – and that's the case with Randolph! He dreamed of playing in the NBA himself as a kid, but the CFL's best goalkeeper in 2018-19 has had a solid footy career for the Republic instead!

BAILEY PEACOCK-FARRELL
NORTHERN IRELAND
Northern Ireland got some great news in 2018 when Peacock-Farrell chose to represent them rather than his country of birth England. He's the youngest GK on this shortlist, so if you see yourself as a manager that wants to help bring through emerging talent, go for BPF!

BEST OF THE REST!
CHECK OUT THESE OTHER SUPERSTARS!

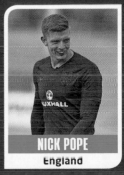

NICK POPE
England

KEIREN WESTWOOD
Republic Of Ireland

SCOTT BAIN
Scotland

DANNY WARD
Wales

NOW PICK YOUR UK AND IRELAND DREAM TEAM GOALKEEPERS!

TURN TO PAGE 52

EURO 2020 DREAM TEAM
CENTRE-BACKS!

JONNY EVANS

NORTHERN IRELAND

You don't rack up over 260 Prem appearances for four different clubs, including over 130 for Man. United, without having top talent – and Evans has still got it! He's never relied on great pace but, instead, possesses a top footy brain to outwit strikers!

CHARLIE MULGREW

SCOTLAND

With natural leader Mulgrew in your squad, you'd barely have to give any team talks – he'd get your team pumped up and ready for games! He's got a real eye for goal, too – he somehow hit 14 league goals for Blackburn in 2017-18, a record for a defender at the club!

SHANE DUFFY

REPUBLIC OF IRELAND

It's been a long journey for the giant Brighton defender, from U21 talent to senior-side sensation! He was called up to the main squad in 2012, but had to wait over two years for his debut. He's since been named ROI's International Player Of The Year in 2017 and 2018!

JAMES LAWRENCE

WALES

We'd never really heard of Lawrence before he was called up to Ryan Giggs' squad in 2018, but he's clearly got some talent! He actually played for Arsenal's youth team alongside Harry Kane, and learnt from Gunners legend Dennis Bergkamp as a kid at Ajax!

JOHN STONES

ENGLAND

You know what you're gonna get with Stones – a classy passer of the ball that will always look to play out from the back rather than smash it long. He can be great to watch, but his style comes with risks – it all depends on the tactics you're planning for your epic squad!

BEST OF THE REST!
CHECK OUT THESE OTHER SUPERSTARS!

CHRIS MEPHAM
Wales

JOE GOMEZ
England

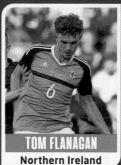
TOM FLANAGAN
Northern Ireland

JOHN EGAN
Republic Of Ireland

STUART FINDLAY
Scotland

ASHLEY WILLIAMS
WALES

The Wales legend, who's in the top three for record appearances for the nation, is fighting for a place in the Wales XI with quality youngster Chris Mepham! The experienced defender was captain of the Dragons side that reached the semi-finals at Euro 2016!

HARRY MAGUIRE
ENGLAND

Of England's two main options, Maguire is much more no-nonsense than Stones. The Man. United hero is actually really good at coming out with the ball as well though, and he's absolutely incredible at aerial duels, so he'll be a massive goal threat from attacking corners!

CRAIG CATHCART
NORTHERN IRELAND

Like his Green and White Army centre-back partner, Jonny Evans, Cathcart came through the youth academy at Man. United – but he never made a PL appearance for them! He was named the Northern Ireland Football Writers' Player Of The Year in May 2019!

RICHARD KEOGH
REPUBLIC OF IRELAND

The dominant Derby defender is a real warrior for his country – he even refused surgery on a broken hand in March 2019 so he wouldn't miss his nation's Euro 2020 qualifiers against Gibraltar and Georgia! You can never have too many leaders in your squad!

SCOTT McKENNA
SCOTLAND

He's only in his early 20s, but MATCH reckons the Aberdeen centre-back is bound to captain his country regularly in the future! He wore the armband for his nation's U19 side, then was handed it in just his fourth senior cap in 2018. A major tourno would be ace experience!

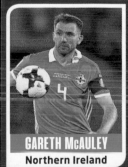
GARETH McAULEY
Northern Ireland

JOHN SOUTTAR
Scotland

KEVIN LONG
Republic Of Ireland

MICHAEL KEANE
England

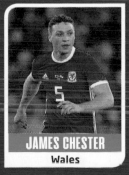
JAMES CHESTER
Wales

NOW PICK YOUR UK AND IRELAND DREAM TEAM CENTRE-BACKS!

TURN TO PAGE 52

EURO 2020 DREAM TEAM
FULL-BACKS!

SEAMUS COLEMAN

REPUBLIC OF IRELAND
Captain Coleman played loads of Gaelic footy as a youngster – a really frantic sport that requires loads of running! We reckon that helped prepare him for a long footy career, because the RB's still got as much lung-busting energy as when he first burst onto the scene!

ANDY ROBERTSON

SCOTLAND
The Scotland captain has proven in the last few years that he's easily one of the best in his position on the planet! He steams up the left-hand side of the pitch, and his directness means that opposition wingers always have to track back – which they hate big time!

KYLE WALKER

ENGLAND
Right-back Walker played in a more central role for England at the 2018 World Cup, but he's spent most of his career bombing up and down the right flank! He's one of the fastest full-backs on the planet, and offers just as much going forward as he does in defence!

BEN DAVIES
WALES
Versatile Tottenham defender Davies' main position is left-back, but he has the ability to play in a back three if you want to switch formations throughout the tournament. He might not be as devastating in attack as some players, but he's a quality all-round defender!

BEN CHILWELL

ENGLAND
One of our favourite did you know facts about Chilwell is that he made his Three Lions debut at his club ground – the first player to do so since Paul Scholes in 1997! He's fairly new to international footy, but has already become his side's regular left-back!

BEST OF THE REST!
CHECK OUT THESE OTHER SUPERSTARS!

DANNY ROSE
England

ENDA STEVENS
Republic Of Ireland

NEIL TAYLOR
Wales

STEPHEN O'DONNELL
Scotland

LUKE SHAW
England

KIERAN TIERNEY
SCOTLAND

When you come to choose your squad later, you'll probably be searching for players that can slot into different positions – like Ben Davies, Kyle Walker and definitely Tierney! Although he prefers playing left-back, the Arsenal superstar can also play at right-back!

MATT DOHERTY
REPUBLIC OF IRELAND

Believe it or not, the flying Wolves wing-back isn't a guaranteed starter for his country with Republic captain Coleman also playing at right-back! We're giving a shout-out to Doherty as well though, after he won us so many FPL points in 2018-19!

JAMAL LEWIS
NORTHERN IRELAND

The youngster is already into double figures for caps for his country, and he's got the potential to reach three digits if he continues his development! Like loads of other candidates you've got to pick from, his main attribute is his pace and ability to drive forward!

CHRIS GUNTER
WALES

Right-back Gunter is a Wales legend! Between 2010 and 2018, he started a mind-boggling 63 matches in a row for The Dragons, and eventually broke Neville Southall's all-time caps record for the country when he made his 93rd Wales appearance in November 2018!

TRENT ALEXANDER-ARNOLD
ENGLAND

We've got to sum up the Liverpool wonderkid in just a few words, so we'll remind you of an epic stat which shows his effectiveness – he got 12 Premier League assists in 2018-19, which is an all-time record for a defender! Do we really need to say any more?

MICHAEL SMITH
Northern Ireland

CONNOR ROBERTS
Wales

KIERAN TRIPPIER
England

CONOR McLAUGHLIN
Northern Ireland

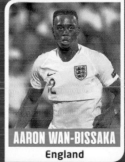
AARON WAN-BISSAKA
England

NOW PICK YOUR UK AND IRELAND DREAM TEAM FULL-BACKS!

TURN TO PAGE 52

EURO 2020 DREAM TEAM
MIDFIELDERS!

AARON RAMSEY
WALES

He's been mega unlucky with injuries throughout his career, but a fully-fit Ramsey has the magic to turn average sides into truly awesome ones! The Juventus superstar knits midfield and attacks together and has the ability to create and bury chances. Legend!

 STEVEN DAVIS

NORTHERN IRELAND

Captain Davis is one of just three stars to have won over 100 caps for Northern Ireland, alongside legendary keeper Pat Jennings and defender Aaron Hughes! His brace v Greece in October 2015 secured his nation's qualification for their first European Championship!

DECLAN RICE
ENGLAND

If you want a defensive midfielder to chomp up opponents' attacks and start your own, look no further! West Ham's Young Hammer Of The Year for the past three seasons will sit in front of your backline and allow you to choose a more attacking midfield partner!

CONOR HOURIHANE
REPUBLIC OF IRELAND

MATCH can't believe the Aston Villa midfielder, who's in his late twenties, has only just won over double figures for international caps! Hourihane was a passenger in the Martin O'Neill era, but is the main man under Mick McCarthy – his runs into the box make him a threat!

 CALLUM McGREGOR

SCOTLAND

The Celtic superstar's been called the 'Marathon Man' by his club's supporters – McGregor was involved in more hours of football in 2018-19 than any other top-flight European player! On average, he played a game every 4.8 days, so he can cope with the hectic Euro schedule!

BEST OF THE REST!
CHECK OUT THESE OTHER SUPERSTARS!

HARRY WINKS
England

ETHAN AMPADU
Wales

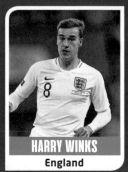
JOHN McGINN
Scotland

PADDY McNAIR
Northern Ireland

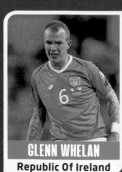
GLENN WHELAN
Republic Of Ireland

DELE ALLI

ENGLAND

Dele's become one of the best Premier League No.10s around, but he started his career as a central midfielder at MK Dons. You can obviously play him where you like, but if you want to use him as a CM, make sure you call up a defensive partner to play with him!

SCOTT McTOMINAY

SCOTLAND

At 6ft 4ins, the Scotland midfielder is a real man mountain in the centre of the pitch! He actually started his youth career as a striker, but works more as a defensive midfielder these days – he'll help keep things simple, while stopping opponents' attacks in the process!

JORDAN HENDERSON

ENGLAND

He hasn't always had the full backing of Three Lions fans, but Henderson is one of those really underrated players – he'll do the scrapping in the middle of the pitch so the 'more exciting' players can work their magic. Plus, he captained Liverpool to the 2019 CL trophy!

JOE ALLEN

WALES

The 'Welsh Xavi', as he's been known in the past, has been out of the Prem spotlight after getting relegated with Stoke in 2018 – but he still plays with the same style! He's a wicked choice if you're a manager that wants to try to dominate possession in matches!

JEFF HENDRICK

REPUBLIC OF IRELAND

Hendrick became Burnley's record signing when he joined for £10.5 million in August 2016, and he's played over 30 Premier League games in each of his first three seasons for The Clarets! He can play as a No.10, out wide or as part of a two-man midfield!

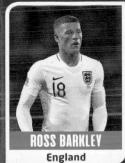

ROSS BARKLEY
England

TOM CAIRNEY
Scotland

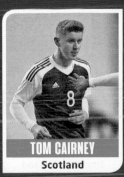

CORRY EVANS
Northern Ireland

A. OXLADE-CHAMBERLAIN
England

RUBEN LOFTUS-CHEEK
England

NOW PICK YOUR UK AND IRELAND DREAM TEAM MIDFIELDERS!

TURN TO PAGE 52

EURO 2020 DREAM TEAM
WINGERS!

JAMES McCLEAN
REPUBLIC OF IRELAND

The Republic winger is a proper grafter – he gives absolutely everything for his nation and never gives up! If he doesn't beat his man at the first attempt, he won't let his head drop – he'll keep plugging away until he skips past him and gets your team an assist!

JADON SANCHO
ENGLAND

As well as grabbing over 25 league goals and assists combined in his first full Bundesliga campaign for Dortmund last season, the ex-Man. City winger also has bags of tricks and flair! He's the sort of player that makes football great fun to watch for supporters!

JORDAN JONES
NORTHERN IRELAND

Jones is a typical winger – he's got a great turn of pace, is a proper direct dribbler and can whip in a fantastic cross into the box! He was Northern Ireland's super sub against Estonia in June 2019, coming on and providing an assist for their winner. Ledge!

DAVID BROOKS
WALES

Brooks was released by Man. City as a youngster, but look at him now! After ripping it up for Sheffield United, he joined Bournemouth and has now established himself in the Prem! We think he prefers playing as a CAM, but he's sick at cutting in off the wing too!

JAMES FORREST
SCOTLAND

The SFWA International Player Of The Year in 2018-19 told MATCH that the most important thing for a winger to succeed is to have loads of confidence and positivity – and Forrest oozes both! It's like his boots are covered with Super Glue the way the ball sticks to his feet!

BEST OF THE REST!
CHECK OUT THESE OTHER SUPERSTARS!

NATHAN REDMOND
England

TOM LAWRENCE
Wales

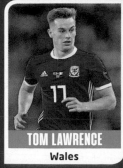

JOHNNY RUSSELL
Scotland

NIALL McGINN
Northern Ireland

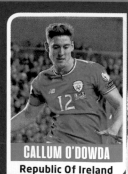

CALLUM O'DOWDA
Republic Of Ireland

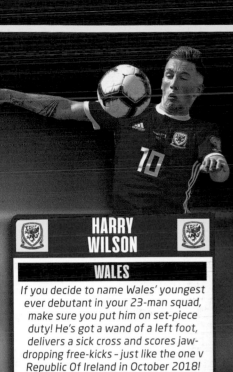

JESSE LINGARD

ENGLAND

Lingard has really announced himself on the international stage since Gareth Southgate took charge – they know each other really well after working together with the under-21s! His long shooting is one of his best weapons – as he proved at World Cup 2018!

HARRY WILSON

WALES

If you decide to name Wales' youngest ever debutant in your 23-man squad, make sure you put him on set-piece duty! He's got a wand of a left foot, delivers a sick cross and scores jaw-dropping free-kicks – just like the one v Republic Of Ireland in October 2018!

RYAN FRASER

SCOTLAND

The 2018-19 Premier League campaign highlighted what a danger Fraser can be! He grabbed 20+ goals and assists combined in a single season for the first time in his career - only Eden Hazard set up more goals than the Scotland wing wizard. Wowzers!

ROBBIE BRADY

REPUBLIC OF IRELAND

The baller has European Championship history! He scored a header v Italy at Euro 2016 to seal a famous win over the mega nation - and see the Republic through to the knockouts! He then hit a penalty against hosts France after just two minutes to show nerves of steel!

CALLUM HUDSON-ODOI

ENGLAND

Hudson-Odoi became the youngest England player ever to win his first cap in a competitive fixture when he came off the bench v Czech Republic in March 2019 – and that was just the start of what will be a sick career for the highly-rated Chelsea winger!

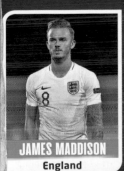

JAMES MADDISON
England

RABBI MATONDO
Wales

ROBERT SNODGRASS
Scotland

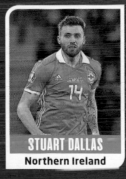

STUART DALLAS
Northern Ireland

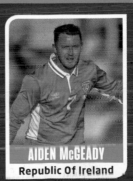

AIDEN McGEADY
Republic Of Ireland

NOW PICK YOUR UK AND IRELAND DREAM TEAM WINGERS!

TURN TO PAGE 52

EURO 2020 DREAM TEAM
FORWARDS!

HARRY KANE
ENGLAND

At his last major international tourno, Kane became the first ever England captain to hit a World Cup hat-trick, and then won the award that every striker dreams of lifting as a kid – the World Cup Golden Boot! On top of that, he's well respected in the dressing room!

OLIVER BURKE
SCOTLAND

Like Bale, Burke's typically known as a winger, but he's been training as a striker over the past 12 months as well! He might not be as lethal as some of the other options you have, but the nippy frontman would create loads of chances for his strike partner!

GARETH BALE
WALES

The Dragons' all-time top scorer can play as a centre-forward, or as one of the widemen in a 4-3-3 formation – but he'll boss either role! He turns 31 just four days after the Euro 2020 final, so he'll be desperate to bag the trophy as an early prezzie - providing you pick him!

DAVID McGOLDRICK
REPUBLIC OF IRELAND

The Sheffield United striker spent five years playing under current Republic gaffer Mick McCarthy at Ipswich earlier in his career, and now they're enjoying working together again! The striker is really good at holding up the ball and bringing other attackers into the game!

CONOR WASHINGTON
NORTHERN IRELAND

The Northern Ireland striker is lucky in that his country's assistant coach Austin MacPhee is also the assistant at his club Hearts, so he probably gets loads of tips on how to impress Green and White Army boss Michael O'Neill – not that he really needs them!

BEST OF THE REST!
CHECK OUT THESE OTHER SUPERSTARS!

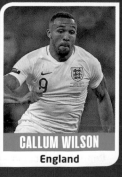

CALLUM WILSON
England

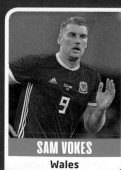

SAM VOKES
Wales

OLI McBURNIE
Scotland

LIAM BOYCE
Northern Ireland

CALLUM ROBINSON
Republic Of Ireland

KYLE LAFFERTY

NORTHERN IRELAND

The giant striker is his country's second-highest all-time top scorer, so if you're after a lethal forward who's proven at international level, Lafferty could be your man! His height makes him a great targetman, so he'd be a perfect choice if you like playing with a lone striker!

DANIEL JAMES

WALES

Lightning-quick forward James is an absolute dream for gaffers wanting to play counter-attacking footy – he was once clocked at running 36km/h, which is basically the same speed as Kylian Mbappe! He mainly plays on the wing, but has been used as a lone forward!

RAHEEM STERLING

ENGLAND

Sterling ended a three-year England goal drought with a match-winning double v Spain in October 2018 – and five months later he'd already doubled his international goal tally with four more net-busters! His Prem stats have been incredible in recent seasons, too!

MARCUS RASHFORD

ENGLAND

Rashford is obviously another option if you're after attacking players with tons of pace! He's become more clinical since teaming up with ex-goal machine Ole Gunnar Solskjaer at Man. United, too – 2018-19 was the first time in his career he reached ten league goals!

SHANE LONG

REPUBLIC OF IRELAND

The Southampton star is one of those forwards that defenders just hate playing against – he's always bustling for loose balls and putting them under pressure! He's won over 80 caps for his country too, so he knows how to impress his international gaffers!

LEIGH GRIFFITHS
Scotland

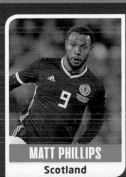

BEN WOODBURN
Wales

MATT PHILLIPS
Scotland

JOSH MAGENNIS
Northern Ireland

SCOTT HOGAN
Republic Of Ireland

NOW PICK YOUR UK AND IRELAND DREAM TEAM FORWARDS!

TURN OVER NOW...

WIN THIS!

CLOSING DATE: JAN. 31 2020

HYPERX

Send us your UK & Ireland Euro 2020 squad and you could win this epic HYPERX CLOUD MIX gaming headset – worn by England hero Dele Alli!

1		9		17	
2		10		18	
3		11		19	
4		12		20	
5		13		21	
6		14		22	
7		15		23	
8		16			

YOU HAVE TO PICK AT LEAST THREE PLAYERS FROM EACH COUNTRY!

Name:

Date of birth:

Address:

Mobile:

Email:

Photocopy this page, fill out your squad and details, then send it to the address below. Winner will be picked at random.
UK & Ireland Dream Team, MATCH Annual 2020, Kelsey Media, Regent House, Welbeck Way, Peterborough, Cambs, PE2 7WH

Fab Fact

Last season saw the Arsenal superstar win only his second ever Golden Boot award!

Boots

Nike Mercurial

Stat Attack

2018-19 was the fourth campaign in a row that Auba had scored 30+ goals in all competitions!

Transfer Value

£80 million

CHAMPIONS LEAGUE
TOP SCORERS BY COUNTRY!

MATCH goes around the world to reveal the all-time Champions League top scorers by country since the competition was re-formatted in 1992!

CENTRAL AMERICA

1	🇲🇽	**Javier Hernandez** *Mexico*	**14** GOALS
2		**Dwight Yorke** *Trinidad & Tobago*	**11** GOALS

SOUTH AMERICA

3		**Lionel Messi** *Argentina*	**112** GOALS
4		**Neymar** *Brazil*	**32** GOALS
5		**Arturo Vidal** *Chile*	**14** GOALS
6		**Jackson Martinez** *Colombia*	**13** GOALS
7		**Oscar Cardozo** *Paraguay*	**11** GOALS
8		**Claudio Pizarro** *Peru*	**21** GOALS
9		**Edinson Cavani** *Uruguay*	**34** GOALS

AFRICA

34		**Samuel Eto'o** *Cameroon*	**30** GOALS
35		**Mohamed Salah** *Egypt*	**18** GOALS
36		**P.E. Aubameyang** *Gabon*	**15** GOALS
37		**Michael Essien** *Ghana*	**11** GOALS
38		**Didier Drogba** *Ivory Coast*	**44** GOALS
39		**George Weah** *Liberia*	**11** GOALS
40		**Sadio Mane** *Senegal*	**14** GOALS
41		**Emmanuel Adebayor** *Togo*	**11** GOALS

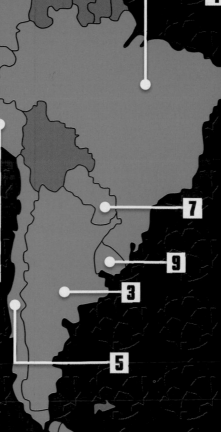

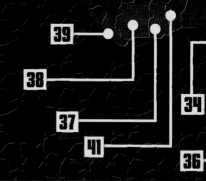

15 22 23 26 33 17 29 25 20 28 12 40 39 38 37 41 34 36

1 2 4 6 7 8 9 3 5

EUROPE

No.	Player	Country	Goals
10	Edin Dzeko	Bosnia & Herz.	22 GOALS
11	Dimitar Berbatov	Bulgaria	13 GOALS
12	Mario Mandzukic	Croatia	21 GOALS
13	Michalis Konstantinou	Cyprus	11 GOALS
14	Pavel Nedved	Czech Republic	15 GOALS
15	Wayne Rooney	England	30 GOALS
16	Jari Litmanen	Finland	23 GOALS
17	Karim Benzema	France	60 GOALS
18	Thomas Muller	Germany	42 GOALS
19	Kostas Mitroglou	Greece	14 GOALS
20	Filippo Inzaghi	Italy	46 GOALS
21	Mirko Vucinic	Montenegro	10 GOALS
22	Ruud van Nistelrooy	Netherlands	56 GOALS
23	Ole Gunnar Solskjaer	Norway	19 GOALS
24	Robert Lewandowski	Poland	53 GOALS
25	Cristiano Ronaldo	Portugal	126 GOALS
26	Roy Keane	Rep. Of Ireland	12 GOALS
27	Dejan Stankovic	Serbia	11 GOALS
28	Zlatko Zahovic	Slovenia	11 GOALS
29	Raul	Spain	71 GOALS
30	Zlatan Ibrahimovic	Sweden	48 GOALS
31	Hakan Sukur	Turkey	13 GOALS
32	Andriy Shevchenko	Ukraine	48 GOALS
33	Ryan Giggs	Wales	28 GOALS

ASIA

42	Heung-Min Son	South Korea	12 GOALS
43	Maksim Shatskikh	Uzbekistan	11 GOALS

VINICIUS JR.
THE NEXT... NEYMAR?

THE KING...

Some forwards are known for getting fans on their feet with wicked tricks and flicks, while others are pure goalscorers, but it takes a special player to be world class at both. Not only is Neymar one of the most skilful footballers on the planet when dribbling at defenders, he's also hit tons of goals for some of the biggest clubs in the world - and he's closing in on Brazil's all-time scoring record too!

THE HEIR...

Full name: *Vinicius Jose Paixao de Oliveira Junior*

D.O.B: *12/07/2000*

Club: *Real Madrid*

Country: *Brazil*

Position: *Winger*

Boots: *Nike Mercurial Vapor*

STORY SO FAR...

Both players began their careers in Brazil before making big-money moves to Spain. But, while Neymar had already grabbed headlines with 136 goals for Santos and more than 30 Brazil caps when he joined Barcelona, nobody had heard of Vinicius when Real announced his signing! They paid £38.7 million to make him the most expensive under-19 star in footy history - and he'd only played one senior match!

PLAYING STYLE!

Like Neymar, Vinicius' favourite position is on the left wing as part of an attacking front three, because it allows him to cut inside on to his stronger right foot to pick out a pass or have a strike at goal. And when it comes to skills, he's got every trick in the book! La Liga defenders have total nightmares about facing Neymar, but now they've got another Brazilian magician to turn them inside out!

HIS IMPACT!

At his best, Neymar was part of the deadliest attacking trio on the planet alongside Lionel Messi and Luis Suarez at Barcelona. After Real Madrid splashed megabucks on Eden Hazard and Luka Jovic in 2019, the Spanish giants are trying to build a deadly front line of their own - and Vinicius has the potential to be a massive part of it! Can they match MSN and fire the Galacticos back to the top of La Liga?

WILL HE RULE?

Vinicius Jr. has made massive progress for a youngster, but he's still got a long way to go to catch Neymar. The Brazil legend was a prolific goalscorer almost as soon as he burst onto the scene at Santos, but Vinicius only scored four times in his first season at Real. If he can add more goals to his game, he'll be one of the best wingers in the world - and could rival Neymar for his place in Brazil's XI!

TOP SKILLS!

DRIBBLING	85
SPEED	93
FLAIR	90
CROSSING	82
SHOOTING	75

LA LIGA HEIRS!

Check out more wonderkids totally ripping it up in Spain...

RODRYGO

The next... Neymar?

Vinicius has only been at the Bernabeu for a year, but Real have signed another wonderkid winger from Brazil nicknamed the 'Next Neymar' too - Rodrygo!

TAKEFUSA KUBO

The next... Lionel Messi?

If Kubo does become the Japanese Messi, Barça will kick themselves - he spent four years in their academy before joining Real!

SAMUEL CHUKWUEZE

The next... Arjen Robben?

The Villarreal and Nigeria young gun has been compared to Robben thanks to his electric pace and ability to cut in off the right wing onto his lethal left foot!

RIQUI PUIG

The next... Andres Iniesta?

Every promising midfielder that comes through Barcelona's youth academy gets compared to the all-time Spain legend!

JUNIOR FIRPO

The next... Jordi Alba?

Alba has bossed Barça's left-back spot for years, but his long-term replacement has been snapped up by the La Liga cham...

BIG MATCH! QUIZ

EFL SPECIAL

on the box!

Which Championship superstar is auditioning on the X Factor?

SPOT THE BALL!

Mark where you think the ball is in this cool action pic!

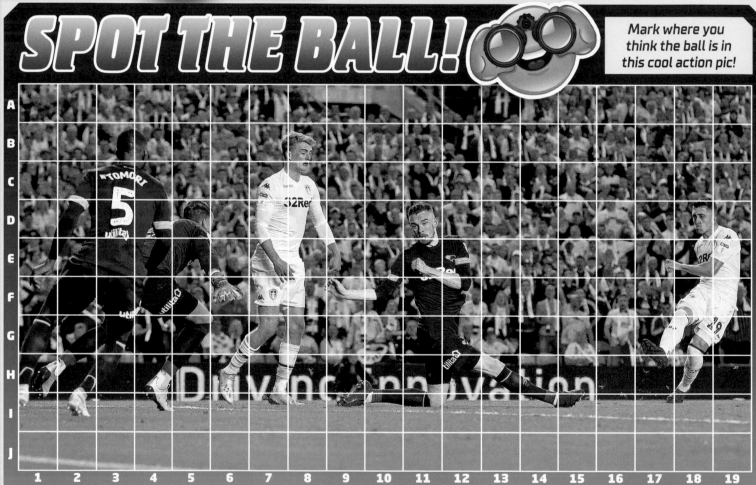

A B C D E F G H I J

1 2 3 4 5 6 7 8 9 10 11 12 13 14 15 16 17 18 19

2018-19

2017-18

GUESS THE WINNERS!

Which teams won the Championship in these seasons?

2016-17

2015-16

FOOTY MIS-MATCH

Spot the ten differences between these two EFL pics!

1		6	
2		7	
3		8	
4		9	
5		10	

ANSWERS ON PAGE 94

MEGA WORDSEARCH

Can you find the 2019-20 EFL heroes hiding in this huge grid?

```
T X N J H I Z                               O W L L H T M
C R O O G N M                               T G Z X U A D
U M R S G M W                               L N A Y T A F
U U W L A O O                               E J B D C Q D
X K O V G W W H I O A K Y C H O G G Y Q V B Z N L M S O E H R A
J Y O S V L Y R D K R G M A R Q U I S F B R Z U D A I R I Q V
W P D G Q G Z E C Z J B P N Q N V K O L N B Z I V F C A B N K I
E N Z W F C T R R M H A T V Q Q K E A C U W F Z Y L A H J S Y E
A S Q V D Q D O V S V J D L J N C M M W W H O A A F I S F O A S
W A M U V C U U T Q Z C X F O K E J A P Z N H S C H R F M N Q Z
S Y P K P I N M E E U E A S R E P E N N Q K G S H X N F G B Y S
M G U A Y L I N G G Y H I R J H R W Z V J E E O F H E K J F J S
V C F E C C B W S S G R M G R R R B D B Z A B M G C Y L O C U G
R N W Z I O R A R M R G E U L O A B I W X I A B F L B M E P G A
T S S Z Z L D O U O M R K F W G L N H G V Z D A C K M A X M A R
O E M U A L M X M Y O Q C F T Q W L S W K K E L L R D Y C H G W
N X Y T H I T F T O L D S E V D I M F M S O A O M M M N V L A L
E F C A B N I H M W E I W C E U W O Q G X F H N W S U A H V R L
Y I M M M S G T I J A G X D G H V D Q Q S R C G K V K R M A D H
H A S A R U M V P C Y V N L E U O S Q L W C J A C M Y D P Z H I
L A V Z O L I H S Z N I E L N O K N G U C L G L D E O F S H W V
N B B D Z S R R T O K D O A Y O U F J Z D J N M L V L C R U Y O
W P B P M O E X S A U S Y W O R L F H A B R I K T B X N R Z E O
I H W X L V F R S V W S G R U G A C K I F R C R T Z S C J B Z K
U X V Y M M E D I U Z R C E Y Z H I N S G O I M I M H M I W U U
Y J A H A D Q F E E M M H N A T G F J V T U P Y A W O T E R S G
U T K K N D D N D Z S O Z C N Q A O M S A N Q I H Q V K S P G X
T H M E Q O S N S J E S I E J L R U G U I P L J Y O W X I S E Z
U M H F O U A Q A K F S U J Q B O K O A L J P B E G G S M U
N X R H G N M D K S P K M N K K U K Y K I P C E F F R R E I L E
C Q R P R U X S I Q R W L U C S T D J W J M R Z T O S E D N X L
G U B E B V C R N L O O Q H Q Z T N R K T O L D D M L A O J F T
P T H G U K U T C A S V N O K G L F V X M C E I J Y V T F K Y W
M L M C V I I C E A S P Q E A V E S E R U U L W E L Y T X T A A
F A K G E W N B J C E Y G S J V V W E W V L D K A M H G X N L
Q D X M R N U Y M K R P Z D M P I V J S W P L K L L M R I Y I K
C A V B F J G K F O M E W J H C I R O B O G Z C N M L B Y W X E
V P F D J Z X G B A A B G H R L T G A U G E F E J F C W A V X R
Y O B A F E X I C T K A M O N D T H U C L D P D T I V Z G X P G
```

Agard	Cairney	Crooks	Eze	Hutchinson	Livermore	Morsy	Stockley
Akinde	Camp	Dack	Garbutt	Ince	Marquis	Murphy	Taylor
Amond	Carroll	Davies	Henderson	Ladapo	Maynard	Norwood	Toney
Assombalonga	Clayton	Doughty	Hernandez	Lawrence	Moore	Prosser	Walker
Ayling	Collins	Eaves	Hogg	Lees	Morrison	Sawyers	Williams

ANSWERS ON PAGE 94

Fab Fact

Rapinoe won the Golden Ball, Golden Boot and Women's World Cup in 2019!

Boots

Nike Mercurial

Stat Attack

Her penalty in the 2019 World Cup final was her 50th international goal for her country. Sick!

Transfer Value

£15 million

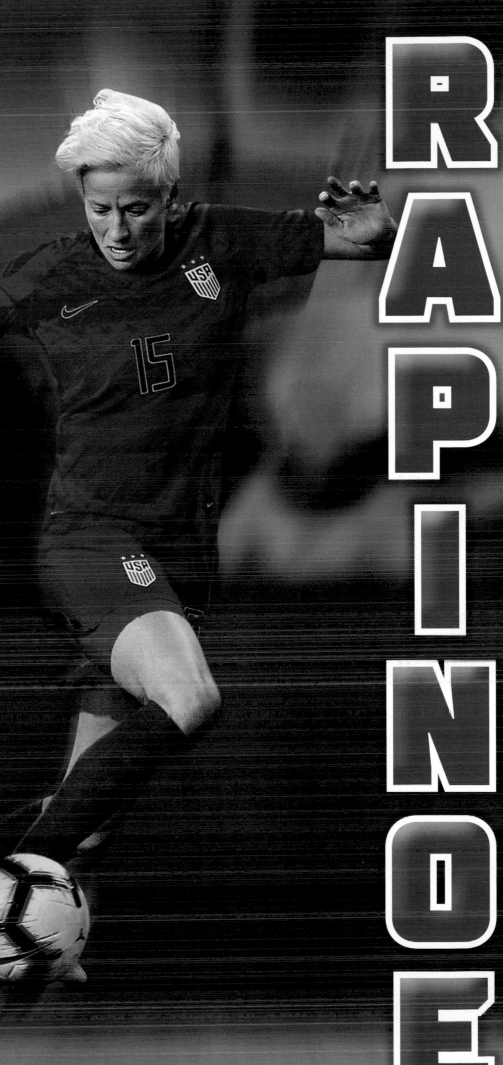

RAPINOE

2019 WOMEN'S WORLD CUP
Scrapbook!

MATCH looks back on the biggest and best moments from last summer's World Cup!

HENRY STUNS SOUTH KOREA!

The host country kicked off the competition in style by smashing South Korea 4-0, thanks to an epic double by defender Wendie Renard and a worldy strike by skipper Amandine Henry!

ITALY'S EPIC COMEBACK!

It doesn't get much more dramatic than a winning goal in the 95th minute! Barbara Bonansea bagged her second goal of the match proper late on as Italy came from 1-0 down to beat Australia 2-1 in Group C!

AULD ENEMIES CLASH!

England's group stage fixture with Scotland caught the eye as soon as the draw was made! The Lionesses bagged a 2-1 victory thanks to Nikita Parris' penalty and a clinical strike by Ellen White!

THAILAND DESTROYED BY USA!

All sorts of records were broken in USA's 13-0 win! Not only was it the biggest victory in World Cup history, Alex Morgan became only the second player to score five goals in one game!

MORE GROUP C MADNESS!

After losing to Italy in their first match, this time Australia were on the other end of a crazy comeback! The Matildas came from 2-0 down to beat Brazil 3-2, sealing the win with an own goal decided by VAR!

FOUR-GOAL KERR!

Australia were on total flames again in their final group match – star player Sam Kerr proved why she's one of the hottest talents on the planet by bagging four goals against Jamaica!

MAGIC MARTA MAKES HISTORY!

Brazil superstar Marta set a new record for career World Cup goals by bagging her 17th from the penalty spot against Italy, overtaking Miroslav Klose's all-time WC record. Legend!

SCOTLAND'S VAR HEARTBREAK!

Scotland had their eye on the knockout stages after taking a 3-0 lead against Argentina, but conceded three goals in the last 20 minutes – including an own goal and an injury-time VAR penalty. Well gutted!

NCHOUT GUNS DOWN NEW ZEALAND!

With both teams needing victory to qualify from Group E, the last ten minutes of Cameroon v New Zealand was crazy! Ajara Nchout sealed the 2-1 win with one of the goals of the tournament after a wicked run!

2019 WOMEN'S WORLD CUP
Scrapbook!

CAMEROON CHAOS!

England's knockout stage 3-0 win over Cameroon was crazy! The African side threatened to walk off after a couple of VAR decisions went against them – firstly when Ellen White's goal was allowed and again when they had a goal disallowed for offside!

SHOOTOUT SHOWDOWN!

The competition's only penalty shootout came after Norway drew 1-1 with Australia in the round of 16! Midfielder Ingrid Engen sunk the winning spot-kick to send The Matildas home!

FRA 1 | 0 BRA 25:34

VAR

EVEN MORE VAR DRAMA!

VAR played a big part in France's game against Brazil too. The hosts eventually won 2-1, but only after a disallowed goal, an overturned offside decision and extra-time!

HERMOSO'S CHEEKY CHIP!

Jenni Hermoso caught USA by surprise and scored one of the goals of the tournament with an epic chip! It wasn't enough for Spain though – they lost 2-1, with Megan Rapinoe scoring two penalty kicks!

BRONZE BAGS AN ABSOLUTE BELTER!

England's place in the semis was never in doubt! Jill Scott scored inside three minutes against Norway in the quarters, Ellen White made it two before half-time and then Lucy Bronze sealed it with a total screamer!

FAVOURITES FACE-OFF!

The hosts meeting the holders was one of the tensest clashes of the tournament! Golden Ball winner Megan Rapinoe was the star, bagging a brace in a 2-1 win, but Wendie Renard's late header made it a nervy finish!

SWEDEN SHOCK THE WORLD!

Two-time champions Germany were stunned by Sweden in the quarter-finals! Nobody expected the Scandinavians to reach the semis, but they beat the Germans 2-1 thanks to net-busters from Sofia Jakobsson and Stina Blackstenius!

FOOTBALL'S STILL NOT COMING HOME!

For the second summer in a row, an England team suffered WC semi-final heartbreak! The Lionesses battled hard against USA – they had a goal ruled out and missed a penalty, but went down 2-1 after goals by deadly forwards Megan Rapinoe and Alex Morgan!

DUTCH DRAMA!

There was more drama in the second semi-final too! Sweden and Netherlands looked set for a goalless draw and a penalty shootout, until Man. United's new signing Jackie Groenen struck in extra-time!

USA ARE CHAMPIONS ONCE MORE!

For the second time in a row, and the fourth time in their history, USA got their hands on the trophy! A penalty from Megan Rapinoe and a solo stunner by Rose Lavelle saw them cruise to a 2-0 victory against the Netherlands – champions!

TOP 10 CRAZY

10 Melbourne Cricket Ground
Australia

Before you scream and shout, we know this ground is normally used for cricket - that's what makes it so weird to see teams playing footy there! While the circular shape of the grass messes with your head a bit, it's cool that over 100,000 people can pack inside - more than at any European footy stadium! Man. City actually took on Real Madrid there in a friendly back in 2015!

8 Mercedes-Benz Stadium
USA

If you're gonna build a new stadium, you might as well make it as modern and high-tech as possible - and that's what Atlanta United chiefs were thinking when they opened the Mercedes-Benz Stadium in 2017! As well as the flower-petal shape roof that allows natural light into the ground, it also boasts the biggest 360-degree HD screens in the footy world!

6 National Stadium
Taiwan

This awesome stadium has been nicknamed 'The Dragon' because it's shaped like the mythical creature's tail and looks like it has scales! What it actually has are over 8,000 layered solar panels, meaning the stadium is 100% powered by sunlight! We're not sure that sort of ground would work so well in the UK...

9 Estadio Hernando Siles
Bolivia

This stadium will take your breath away - literally! The Bolivia national team's home is located more than 3,600 metres above sea level, so it's one of the highest in the world! Players struggle to breathe because of the low oxygen levels - Lionel Messi was actually sick on the pitch back in 2013 because he was suffering so much from the altitude. Bonkers!

7 Stadion Vozdovac
Serbia

Have you ever gone to a footy match and realised you've left your packed lunch or an extra layer of clothing at home? At FK Vozdovac Belgrade's ground that's no issue! The 5,175-capacity stadium was actually built on top of a shopping centre, so you can do your weekly shop after the match - or even during it if the game turns out to be a proper snoozefest. Just don't leave your wallet at home!

5 Estadio Municipal De Braga
Portugal

This is the only stadium on this list currently being used by a team in a major European league - Sporting Braga in Portugal's Primeira Division! The crazy ground, which was built for the 2004 European Championship and holds 30,000 fans, was carved into the side of a mountain - with the scoreboard mounted on a cliff at the edge of the stadium. Minds blown...

STADIUMS!

4

Estadio Janguito Malucelli
Brazil

This crazy ground is known as the Ecostadium, after being built in 2007 without any concrete and only natural, eco-friendly products! The first-ever 'green' stadium in Brazil has seats for fans dug into the ground on top of a hill. Not recommended if you want a luxurious matchday experience!

3

Igraliste Batarija
Croatia

You'll often hear fans calling their home stadium a 'fortress', but for HNK Trogir supporters in Croatia, it really is! Their ground was built in between two protected monuments – a tower that formed part of the old city walls and an ancient castle! Unfortunately for the home team, there isn't a moat surrounding their goal or knights in armour protecting the goalmouth...

2

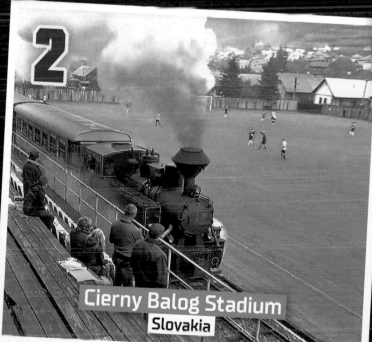

Cierny Balog Stadium
Slovakia

If there are any keen train spotters among you, this one's for you! The Cierny Balog Stadium, home to TJ Tatran Cierny in Slovakia, was built alongside a train track, with old steam trains passing directly in front of the stand where the fans sit. As far as we know, supporters don't pay less for an obstructed view!

1

The Float At Marina Bay
Singapore

It's pretty clear where this ground got its name from – it's the world's largest floating stage and MATCH's craziest stadium in the world! It's not used very often as a football pitch, except for the odd amateur game, and we can guess why. You'd need to take tons of balls, because you won't be getting them back easily if they get smashed over the fence – unless your ball boys like a swim!

TURN OVER TO DESIGN YOUR OWN STADIUM! ▶

DRAW YOUR OWN GROUND!

Now you've seen some of the world's weirdest stadiums, have a go at designing your own! Try to think of at least three things that will make it unique, then get scribbling!

Name:

Date of birth:

Address:

Mobile:

Email:

EUROPE'S...
SUPER CLUBS!

MATCH reveals the most successful European clubs based on all-time trophies won!

HOW IT WORKS The list only includes clubs that have won a major European trophy, and does not include non top-flight league titles or lower league cup trophies.

10TH — MAN. UNITED

The Red Devils edge out Liverpool, Anderlecht, Red Star Belgrade, Dynamo Kiev and Galatasaray to sneak into the top 10! They've won a record 20 English league titles and are the only club from England to win the league, domestic cup and Champions League treble!

TROPHIES 66

9TH — JUVENTUS

Juventus bagged their eighth Serie A title in a row in 2018-19, and a record 35th Italian championship overall - nearly double the 18 victories of their nearest rivals Inter and AC Milan! They'd be even higher in this list if it wasn't for losing a record SEVEN Champions League finals!

TROPHIES 67

8TH — AJAX

One of football's most iconic clubs returned to the big-time in 2018-19 after winning the Dutch double and reaching the Champo League semi-finals! Ajax are one of only four sides to win the treble, plus all three major UEFA crowns - the Champions League, Europa League and Cup Winners' Cup!

TROPHIES 71

7TH — BAYERN MUNICH

Bayern are the kings of German footy! They've won 29 league titles - no other club has reached double figures, plus 19 German Cups - no other club has won more than six! Their trophy cabinet also includes the Champions League, Intercontinental Cup and FIFA Club World Cup!

TROPHIES 72

6TH — PORTO

Porto have won 28 league titles and 20 Portuguese cups but, incredibly, those aren't even national records! They do hold one major bragging right over their biggest Portuguese rivals, though - they've won seven continental crowns in total, including two Champions Leagues. Legends!

TROPHIES 76

5TH — BENFICA

The record for Portuguese league and cup wins goes to Lisbon giants Benfica - they've won 37 Primeira Ligas and 26 Portuguese cups to edge out Porto! Added to that the two European Cups they bagged in the 1960s, and Benfica can proudly call themselves the kings of Portuguese footy!

TROPHIES 83

4TH — REAL MADRID

No team has won more Spanish titles than Real Madrid - an epic 33 crowns - but Los Blancos' international record is even more special! A record 13 Champions League trophies, including four in the past six years, plus four FIFA Club World Cups are what set them apart from the rest of Europe!

TROPHIES 90

3RD — BARCELONA

Barça haven't won as many La Ligas, Champo Leagues or Club World Cups as arch enemies Real, but they're ahead of their Clasico rivals on total trophies won thanks to an epic 30 Copa del Rey victories! That's helped them win eight domestic doubles in total - double Madrid's tally of four!

TROPHIES 94

2ND — CELTIC

The Bhoys have won the last eight Scottish titles to take their overall tally to an eye-popping 50 in total, including the treble treble - all three major Scottish domestic trophies in 2017, 2018 and 2019! They were also the first British club ever to win the European Cup way back in 1967!

TROPHIES 108

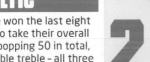
BIG BOYS!

1ST — RANGERS

Rangers haven't won a top-flight title or cup competition since 2011, but that doesn't stop them from being the most decorated club in Europe! No team has won more than their 54 league titles, while they've also won 60 domestic cup trophies combined, plus the European Cup Winners' Cup!

TROPHIES 115

Only includes trophies won prior to the start of 2019-20.

BIG MATCH! QUIZ

LEGENDS SPECIAL

GAME CHANGER!

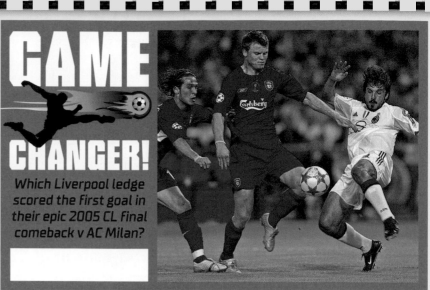

Which Liverpool ledge scored the first goal in their epic 2005 CL Final comeback v AC Milan?

THE NUMBERS GAME!

How many Champions League trophies did Xavi win at Barcelona?

TROPHY TIME!

Which Prem legend is hiding behind the PL trophy?

ONE-CLUB HEROES!

Which Prem sides did these legends play their entire pro careers at?

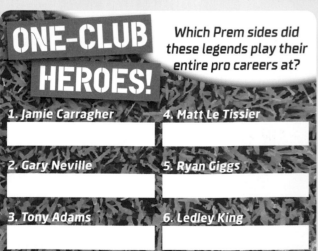

1. Jamie Carragher

2. Gary Neville

3. Tony Adams

4. Matt Le Tissier

5. Ryan Giggs

6. Ledley King

Cafu	David Beckham	Oliver Kahn	Paolo Maldini

ODD ONE OUT!

Which of these heroes didn't win over 100 caps for their country?

Thierry Henry

Diego Simeone

MEGA MASH-UP!

Can you name the footy ledge in this weird pic?

ACTION REPLAY

How much do you know about the 2006 World Cup final between Italy and France?

1 Who did France beat in the semis to reach the final – Portugal or Germany?

2 In what country was the epic tournament held?

3 Which legendary Les Bleus midfielder scored the opener from the penalty spot – Patrick Vieira or Zinedine Zidane?

4 Which Italy CB scored in the 19th minute – Materazzi or Cannavaro?

5 The match went to extra-time, but what was the score at the full-time whistle?

6 How did Zinedine Zidane get sent off in extra-time – a lunge, a handball, arguing with the ref or a headbutt?

7 Which France ace missed in the penalty shootout – Sylvain Wiltord, David Trezeguet or Eric Abidal?

8 And which Italian scored the winning kick – Alessandro Del Piero or Fabio Grosso?

9 True or False? Zidane never played another match for Les Bleus!

ANSWERS ON PAGE 94

LEGENDS WORDFIT!

Can you fit 30 total legends into this grid?

Baggio	Ginola	Maradona
Ballack	Gullit	Nakata
Baresi	Hagi	Okocha
Bergkamp	Henry	Pele
Best	Keane	Pires
Cruyff	Klose	Puyol
Deco	Kluivert	Ronaldo
Ferdinand	Larsson	Shevchenko
Figo	Laudrup	Veron
Giggs	Litmanen	Zola

P I R E S

ANSWERS ON PAGE 94

Fab Fact

When Aston Villa signed the massive fans' favourite, they #AnnouncedMings at the train station!

Boots

Nike Tiempo

Stat Attack

Tyrone Mings' combined career transfer fees to Bournemouth and then to Aston Villa total almost £30 million!

Transfer Value

£25 million

MINGS

RODRI
THE NEXT...
SERGIO BÜSQUETS?

THE KING...

Sergio Busquets has been controlling games for Barcelona and Spain ever since he first appeared at the Nou Camp back in 2008. He doesn't blow opponents away with incredible athleticism or breathtaking goals, but he can outthink anybody - and he's got the honours to prove it. In total, he's won over 100 Spain caps and more than 30 major titles, including the World Cup, Euros, three CL trophies and eight La Ligas - and he's far from finished!

THE HEIR...

Full name: *Rodrigo Hernandez Cascante*

D.O.B: *23/06/1996*

Club: *Man. City*

Country: *Spain*

Position: *Defensive midfielder*

Boots: *Nike PhantomVSN*

STORY SO FAR...

Rodri joined hometown club Atletico Madrid when he was 11, but was released after six years for being too weak. He moved on to Villarreal and progressed through their ranks and, in 2018, Atletico splashed out close to £20 million to re-sign him! The Spanish side slapped a £62.8 million buyout clause in his contract to prevent clubs from chasing him, but it wasn't enough to stop the English champions from snapping him up in 2019!

PLAYING STYLE!

If you've seen Rodri playing for Spain, we'd forgive you for mistaking him for Busquets, because their styles are identical! The lanky midfielders are masters at winning the ball back and were both among La Liga's top five tacklers in 2018-19. When they get it, they play a simple pass to a team-mate, they're always available to receive possession and, if they get closed down, their feet are quick enough to dribble themselves out of trouble!

HIS IMPACT!

As a player, Pep Guardiola was the ultimate holding midfielder, so when he became Barça boss in 2008, one of his first moves was to promote Busquets to the first team. With Xavi and Andres Iniesta alongside him, Barcelona controlled games and won two Champions Leagues. Now Pep is hoping Rodri can do the same at Man. City and, with David Silva and Kevin De Bruyne alongside him, the champs' midfield trio could be just as good as Barça's!

WILL HE RULE?

Without the coaching of Guardiola, Busquets would never have become the legendary midfielder that he is now, so the Man. City boss is the perfect manager for Rodri. He's got a long way to go to match the king's achievements, but Spain definitely don't need to stress over who's gonna boss their midfield for the next decade – Rodri's got it!

TOP SKILLS!

TACKLING		89
INTERCEPTING		82
POSITIONING		84
PASSING		86
TECHNIQUE		80

PREM HEIRS!

Check out more wonderkids ripping it up in England...

CALLUM HUDSON-ODOI
The next... Eden Hazard?

Chelsea supporters can forget all about Hazard if their homegrown hero fulfils his potential – the direct dribbler could be a world-class winger in a few years!

SEAN LONGSTAFF
The next... Steven Gerrard?

The Newcastle midfielder could become his boyhood club's main man in central midfield for years to come – just like Steven Gerrard was for Liverpool!

PHIL FODEN
The next... David Silva?

Legendary Spain playmaker Silva is set to leave Man. City in 2020, and Foden could be the hero to fill his gigantic boots!

MASON GREENWOOD
The next... Marcus Rashford?

Rashford is only four years older than Greenwood! The pair of them could form an awesome homegrown partnership for Man. United in a few seasons' time!

REISS NELSON
The next... Alexis Sanchez?

Arsenal never replaced their old winger, but Nelson's pace, energy and goal threat mean he's got all the tools to be a really devastating attacker for The Gunners!

MESSI V RONALDO!

MATCH checks out why BARCELONA superstar LIONEL MESSI should be crowned the GOAT!

40+ GOAL MACHINE!

Leo's the only player in history to score over 40 club goals in all competitions in ten consecutive campaigns – from 2009-10 to 2018-19! Now you can't get more consistent than that!

LA LIGA LEGEND!

He holds a ridiculous amount of La Liga records, but the most important are probably the fact he's the league's all-time top scorer, has bagged more assists than any other player and has won more matches than anyone!

CLASICO KING!

El Clasico between Barcelona and Real Madrid is easily one of the biggest and most-watched matches on the planet, so to be the all-time top scorer in the fixture's history is a huge deal! Congrats, Leo!

GOLDEN SHOE STAR!

The European Golden Shoe is awarded to the leading goalscorer in all of Europe's top divisions, and Messi's won the prize six times – twice more than C-Ron and more than anybody else!

GETAFE GOAL!

The incredible dribbler scored one of the greatest goals of all time back in 2007 against Getafe! He received the ball in his own half, skinned four defenders and the goalkeeper, before dinking it over a player on the line!

GUINNESS WORLD RECORD!

One of our fave Messi facts is his Guinness World Record for the most official goals in a calendar year! He scored a mind-boggling 91 times in 69 games for Barcelona and Argentina in 2012!

ARGENTINA ACE!

Who cares if Messi never wins anything with Argentina, he's still their all-time record scorer with over 65 goals, their third all-time appearance maker and holds the record for most all-time Copa America assists!

BARÇA BEAST!

Fans complain loads about player loyalty, but you can't get much more loyal than Leo! Barcelona's all-time top scorer is the only player in history to score 600 goals for a single club - and has won a record number of trophies for them, too!

CL TON-UP!

Ronaldo might be the record Champions League goalscorer, but Leo was the fastest to reach 100 CL goals! He's also got a better goal-to-game ratio in the competition than any other player who's scored over 50. Ledge!

MESSI v RONALDO!

There are strong arguments for CRISTIANO RONALDO to be named the greatest of all time, too!

CHAMPO LEAGUE KING!

Cristiano's busted more Champo League nets than any other player, bagged more Champo League top scorer prizes and holds the record for most goals in a single CL season – 17!

50+ GOAL MACHINE!

Messi holds the record for consistently scoring over 40 club goals, but Cristiano is the only player in history to have scored more than 50 goals in six straight seasons – from 2010-11 to 2015-16. Wow!

BIG-GAME PLAYER!

On top of all his other scoring records in the Champions League, he's also netted four goals in five CL finals and lifted five trophies for Real Madrid and Man. United – both records!

OVERHEAD KICK STAR!

He's a Juventus hero now, but in 2017-18 CR7 broke their hearts by scoring one of the greatest goals ever – an incredible overhead kick, which was voted UEFA's best goal that season!

PORTUGAL POWERS!

As well as being Portugal's all-time top goalscorer and record appearance maker, CR7 is second on the all-time international top scorers chart, with Iran's Ali Daei the only player ahead of him on 109 goals!

EUROS CHAMP!

At Euro 2016, not only did CR7 help Portugal to the trophy, he also equalled the record for most all-time goals at European Championships, became the outright all-time appearance maker and became the first player to score at four different tournaments!

INTERNATIONAL ICON!

Unlike his mega rival Messi, Cristiano has captained his country to their only two major trophies in history – the 2016 European Championship and the 2019 Nations League!

LA LIGA BALLER!

Leo might be the Spanish league's all-time top scorer, but no player in La Liga history who's scored over 100 goals has a better goal-to-game ratio than Cristiano – he netted 311 times in 292 games!

3-LEAGUE LEGEND!

While Leo's chosen to stay in La Liga his entire career, Cristiano made history in 2019 by becoming the first player ever to win league titles in England, Spain and Italy!

HOW THEY SCORED 600 CLUB GOALS!

MESSI and RONALDO both hit the 600-club goal landmark in 2019 – let's compare how the two superstars did it!

HEAD	
MESSI	22
RONALDO	104

LEFT FOOT	
MESSI	491
RONALDO	110

RIGHT FOOT	
MESSI	85
RONALDO	384

OTHER	
MESSI	2
RONALDO	2

PENALTIES	
MESSI	70
RONALDO	102

FREE-KICKS	
MESSI	42
RONALDO	46

Ronaldo reached the landmark first, but Leo did it in 118 fewer games!

MATCH!
THE BEST FOOTBALL MAGAZINE!

Fab Fact

When Puma released the Anthem Pack, they created an album cover of Kun for his playlist!

Boots

Puma ONE

Stat Attack

No player has scored more all-time Premier League hat-tricks than the Man. City legend!

Transfer Value

£80 million

AGUERO

Legendary PREM No.7s!

ARSENAL

ROBERT PIRES 7

When 1998-double winning hero Marc Overmars left The Gunners in 2000, Arsenal fans were worried how they'd replace him – but they ended up signing an even better player! 'Bobby' Pires, as he was affectionately known, scored one of the best goals in Prem history against Aston Villa in 2002 when he lobbed Peter Schmeichel, before netting an FA Cup final winner in 2003 and helping The Gunners become 'Invincibles' in 2003-04! After the silky winger left the club in 2006, he was voted Arsenal's sixth greatest player of all time!

CAREER PREM STATS

Games	Goals	Wins
198	62	115

ASTON VILLA

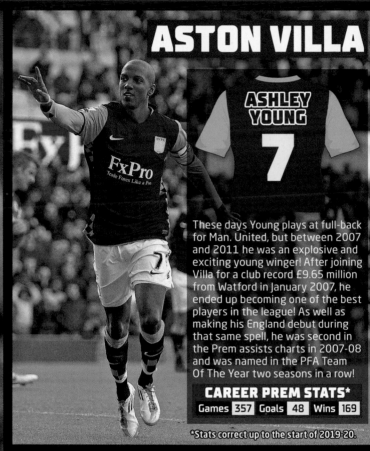

ASHLEY YOUNG 7

These days Young plays at full-back for Man. United, but between 2007 and 2011 he was an explosive and exciting young winger! After joining Villa for a club record £9.65 million from Watford in January 2007, he ended up becoming one of the best players in the league! As well as making his England debut during that same spell, he was second in the Prem assists charts in 2007-08 and was named in the PFA Team Of The Year two seasons in a row!

CAREER PREM STATS*

Games	Goals	Wins
357	48	169

*Stats correct up to the start of 2019-20.

BLACKBURN

STUART RIPLEY 7

When Blackburn won the Prem title in 1994-95, it was mainly down to their lethal 'SAS' strikeforce of Alan Shearer and Chris Sutton, but Ripley played a major role too! The winger got 45 career Prem assists – and most were for Shearer and Sutton! His crossing was class and, although he wasn't known for his goalscoring, he did actually score Blackburn's first-ever Prem goal back in 1992!

CAREER PREM STATS

Games	Goals	Wins
240	14	111

CHELSEA

N'GOLO KANTE
7

Midfield machine N'Golo Kante had already won the Prem title with Leicester before repeating the trick and bagging the PFA Player Of The Year award too in his debut season at Stamford Bridge! The Blues' No.7 shirt was cursed for years – players with big reputations never lived up to the hype... Andriy Shevchenko, Adrian Mutu, Didier Deschamps and Maniche to name a few, while some stunk it out altogether – you have to whisper Winston Bogarde's name around Stamford Bridge! But now the France World Cup-winning star wears it, Blues fans love snapping up shirts with No.7 on the back!

CAREER PREM STATS*
Games	142	Goals	7	Wins	89

*Stats correct up to the start of 2019-20.

EVERTON

GRAHAM STUART
7

Attacker Stuart had decent spells at Chelsea, Sheffield United and Charlton, but he's mostly know for his time at Everton where he was nicknamed 'Diamond! Originally he wore the No.8 shirt before getting his fave No.7, and he was part of two moments that will live in the Goodison faithful's hearts forever! Firstly, on the last Premier League day in 1994 when he scored twice v Wimbledon to save the club from relegation, and then in the 1995 FA Cup final when Paul Rideout's header sank Man. United after Stuart's shot had hit the bar!

CAREER PREM STATS
Games	294	Goals	45	Wins	86

LEICESTER

NEIL LENNON
7

Before Leicester caused one of the biggest upsets ever by winning the title in 2015-16, they had another famous side that rocked the Premier League in the '90s – and Lennon was pivotal to that team! Under gaffer Martin O'Neill, The Foxes upset all the odds by finishing in the top half of the table four seasons in a row, as well as winning two League Cups – and the intelligence of midfielder Lennon was key to their success! He eventually followed manager O'Neill to Scottish giants Celtic in 2000, but not before securing his place as a proper Foxes legend!

CAREER PREM STATS
Games	155	Goals	5	Wins	59

ROBBIE KEANE

7

Republic Of Ireland legend Keane smashed in 126 Prem goals during his career, taking him up to 15th on the all-time scoring charts! Most of those strikes came for Tottenham in the No.10 shirt, but he burst on to the Prem scene in the No.7 jersey as a teenager at Coventry, and then totally owned the shirt number for a season and a half at Leeds, as The Whites challenged the best teams in England and Europe!

CAREER PREM STATS

| Games | 349 | Goals | 126 | Wins | 139 |

LEEDS

MAN. UNITED

LIVERPOOL

LUIS SUAREZ

7

Liverpool's No.7 shirt is truly iconic! Winger Steve McManaman rocked it in the early Prem era, while arguably The Reds' best ever player Kenny Dalglish made it famous in the '70s and '80s. However, not many players have made as much of an impact at Anfield as Suarez! His ratio of 0.63 goals per game is one of the best in Prem history, and his 31 in 2013-14 almost fired the club to the title!

CAREER PREM STATS

| Games | 110 | Goals | 69 | Wins | 53 |

GEORGI KINKLADZE

7

Man. City supporters have a truly world-class hero donning the No.7 shirt these days in Raheem Sterling, but any City fan who remembers Kinkladze play will tell you he was just as talented! He only wore the No.7 jersey for one season in the Prem before suffering relegation in 1995-96, but his twinkle-toed dribbling totally lit up matches!

CAREER PREM STATS

| Games | 102 | Goals | 7 | Wins | 22 |

MAN. CITY

GEORGE BOATENG

7

A lot of No.7s on this list were magicians with the ball at their feet, but Boateng was a different sort of footballer! The midfielder was a tough tackler, had bags of energy and was never afraid to put his body on the line! After decent spells at Coventry and Aston Villa, it was at Middlesbrough where the Dutch international really made his mark. He played over 180 Premier League games in their No.7 shirt between 2002 and 2008, and also won the 2004 League Cup – his only major trophy in English football!

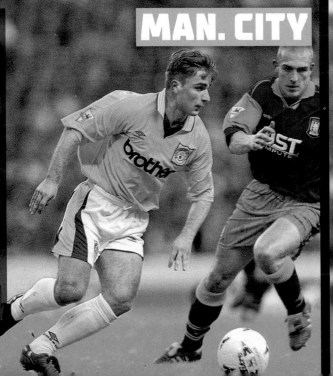

CAREER PREM STATS

| Games | 384 | Goals | 17 | Wins | 125 |

ERIC CANTONA
7

'King Eric' is regarded as one of The Red Devils' greatest ever players - not many stars single-handedly won games and league titles like Cantona did for the club! David Beckham and Cristiano Ronaldo would go on to wear the No.7 shirt after Cantona, but even those two megastars struggled to match his individual genius! On top of his 70 Prem goals, he also got 56 assists, and Sir Alex Ferguson said he was one of only four world-class players he managed at United - along with CR7, Paul Scholes and Ryan Giggs'

CAREER PREM STATS

Games	156	Goals	70	Wins	94

ROBERT LEE
7

While a lot of Newcastle fans say that their favourite player of all time is Alan Shearer or Andy Cole, tons of The Toon Army supporters have a massive soft spot for Lee! The box-to-box midfield machine was one of the best players in the Premier League in the 1990s, and was an integral part of The Magpies' team that nearly won the league title in 1995-96 under manager Kevin Keegan! His energy, passing and long shooting totally rocked!

CAREER PREM STATS

Games	280	Goals	34	Wins	129

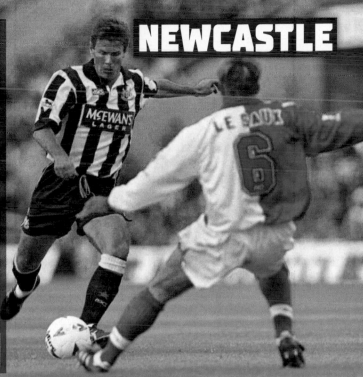

NEWCASTLE

SOUTHAMPTON

MATT LE TISSIER
7

If 'one-club man' was in the football dictionary, Le Tissier would be the definition! 'Le God' was linked with the likes of Man. United at his peak, but he stayed loyal to The Saints his entire pro career! As well as being famous for tricks and wondergoals, he also bagged 64 assists and was a penalty expert, scoring 47 out of 48 spot-kicks during his career!

CAREER PREM STATS

Games	270	Goals	100	Wins	80

MIDDLESBRO'

NICK BARMBY
7

Barmby is one of only nine players to score for six teams in the Prem! He starred for Leeds, Liverpool, Hull, Middlesbrough and Everton, but it was as a highly-rated wonderkid at Tottenham between 1992 and 1995 where he really shone wearing the No.7 shirt! As well as bagging 53 career Prem goals, the ex-England international also got 50 assists!

CAREER PREM STATS

Games	343	Finals	53	Wins	99

TOTTENHAM

#TRENDING

MATCH has picked out its favourite social media LOLs from 2019!

AS Roma English ✓
@ASRomaEN

The one they all wanted to win! 🌳💪😂

#ASRoma #RomaReal #MabelGreenCup

TROPH-TREE!

Forget about the Champions League, Roma's Twitter was more excited about winning the Mabel Green Cup – and its mad tree-shaped trophy!

S-MASH-ING KIT!

Hull's tiger-print shirt and Arsenal's bruised banana strip rock, but this bangers-and-mash kit from non-league's Bedale is our fave of 2019!

Southampton FC ✓
@SouthamptonFC

The Ralph Express rolls on! 🕵️

Departing: Birmingham
Destination: Southampton

Welcome aboard, @CheAdams_!
#saintsfc

SILLY SAINTS!

A spying Jurgen Klopp appeared in Southampton's official Che Adams signing reveal video, because Liverpool always try to sign their best players. LOL!

Manchester City ✓ @ManCity
¯_(ツ)_/¯

'JHON' DE BRUYNE?

MATCH was well confused by this snap of Man. City superstar Kevin De Bruyne carrying a coffee cup with the name 'Jhon' on it! What's that all about, Kev?

MASCOT MADNESS!

The award to the most bonkers – and tastiest – mascot of the year definitely goes to Wigan's Crusty... it's a giant pie! Steak and kidney or chicken and mushroom?

PORKY 'POOS'!

James Maddison's reaction to transfer gossip and Harry Maguire's big-money move to Man. United had MATCH in stitches! Was Maguire telling Madds porkies all along?

James Maddison ✓
@Madders10

He's got the 💩💩💩 🤢

Sky Sports News ✓ @SkySportsNews
BREAKING: Harry Maguire didn't take part in Leicester City training today, amid continued interest in him from Manchester United.

10:25 am · 29 Jul 2019

FACE-APP FUNNIES!

We couldn't get enough of the FaceApp trend when teams transformed their stars into old men! We reckon Harry Kane will still be busting nets in his old age!

XMAS' NO.1 FAN!

This might just look like a standard pic of Bernardo Silva's Xmas tree... but he uploaded it in May! That's either super prepared or mega lazy!

bernardocarvalhosilva
Manchester, United Kingdom

Le gusta a **bakayoko_official14** y 85.715 personas más
bernardocarvalhosilva Bad luck?? 😤 It's staying up!!!

FELIPE'S FRO!

West Ham used this poster of hero Felipe Anderson to promote their pre-season tour in China, but it looked like the Brazilian had a never-ending Afro. LOL!

FAN FAIL!

You can stop rubbing your eyes – this really is a Man. United fan with Aguero on his shirt! Turns out it was his actual name. Poor guy!

JADON SANCHO!

THE NEXT... RAHEEM STERLING?

THE KING...

Raheem Sterling has been a PL star since 2012, so it's easy to forget he's still in his mid-20s! In his short career, he's already appeared for two of the biggest clubs in England, played over 300 games, racked up more than 100 Prem goals and assists combined, and in 2019 he won his 50th England cap! The forward is one of the biggest sporting heroes in the country – and he's only going to get bigger. Ledge!

THE HEIR...

Full name: *Jadon Malik Sancho*
D.O.B: *25/03/2000*
Club: *Borussia Dortmund*
Country: *England*
Position: *Winger*
Boots: *Nike Mercurial Superfly*

STORY SO FAR...

Sterling was only 15 when Liverpool signed him from QPR's academy, and Sancho made a similar move to a Premier League giant a year younger. He left Watford's academy to join Man. City, and made his name as one of the most talented teenagers around. But, while Sterling was given his chance in the Prem at the age of 17 by The Reds, Sancho joined Dortmund for £8 million in 2017 – and was handed their No.7 jersey straight away!

PLAYING STYLE!

When he first burst onto the scene, Sterling tormented Prem defenders with his speed and dribbling, and Sancho is the same – the hero completed more dribbles than any other Bundesliga player in 2018-19! The Man. City star is just as good without the ball and bags loads of tap-ins because his movement is so good – and Sancho's copying that part of his game too. Eleven of the trickster's 12 league goals last season came from inside the box!

HIS IMPACT!

Raheem played a huge role in the Liverpool side that just missed out on the Prem title in 2013-14, but chose to leave for the chance to win silverware. Sancho was on flames as Dortmund led the Bundesliga for most of last season, but they still finished second, so he might have to move for major trophies too. Sterling's £50 million transfer made him the most expensive English player ever in 2015, but Jadon's fee could be worth double that!

WILL HE RULE?

2018-19 was only Sancho's second senior season, yet he bagged double figures for both goals and assists - something that Sterling didn't achieve until 2017-18! He's already well on track to be as good as the Man. City man, and there's a good chance these two will be lining up on either side of England's attack for years to come - and getting on the end of each other's crosses!

TOP SKILLS!

DRIBBLING		84
TRICKS		89
SPEED		88
MOVEMENT		81
FINISHING		78

BUNDESLIGA HEIRS!

Check out more wonderkids ripping it up in Germany...

RABBI MATONDO

The next... Jadon Sancho?

The Wales winger followed Sancho by leaving Man. City for the Bundesliga! Can he repeat the England man's success and rip it up for German giants Schalke?

ALPHONSO DAVIES

The next... Arjen Robben?

After their legendary left-footer retired, Bayern will be hoping the Canadian wonderkid can fill Robben's boots!

JONATHAN TAH

The next... Jerome Boateng?

Boateng's time with Germany is over but, in Leverkusen defender Tah, they've got a CB that's good enough to replace him!

IBRAHIMA KONATE

The next... Raphael Varane?

France have got loads of world-class centre-backs right now, but Konate and his RB Leipzig team-mate Dayot Upamecano are the next generation!

KAI HAVERTZ

The next... Toni Kroos?

Kroos started his career as an attacking midfielder at Bayer Leverkusen as well! Can Havertz match his top potential?

WIN!

LOVE MATCH?
GET IT DELIVERED EVERY WEEK!

FREE 15 EURO GOAL KING POSTERS!

15 EURO GOAL KING POSTERS!

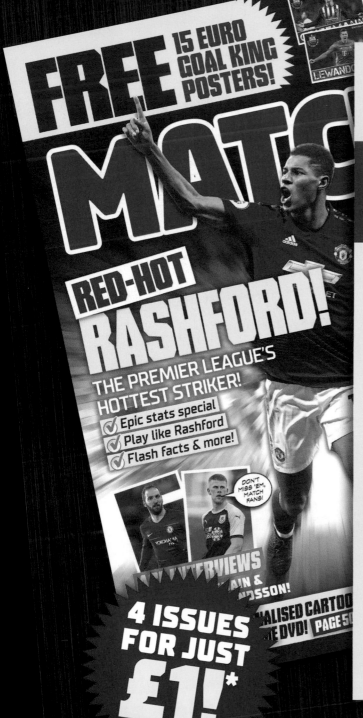

MATCH

RED-HOT RASHFORD!

THE PREMIER LEAGUE'S HOTTEST STRIKER!

- ✓ Epic stats special
- ✓ Play like Rashford
- ✓ Flash Facts & more!

DON'T MISS 'EM, MATCH FANS!

...ERVIEWS ...AIN & ...DSSON!

...ALISED CARTOO... ...IE DVD! PAGE 5...

4 ISSUES FOR JUST £1!*

GIFTS! PREM TEAM GUIDE!

NEW KIT SPECIAL! EVERY PREM CLUB'S SHIRT!

JOELINTON Newcastle's £40 million Goal King

DOUBLE ISSUE!

AUGUST 6-19, 2019 ◆ ISSUE: 2035 | 32 | £2.99

9 770965 494988

MATCH!

》INSIDE! 》INSIDE!

PREMIER LEAGUE

TEAM GUIDES 2019-20

YOUR ULTIMATE GUIDE TO ALL 20 PREM CLUBS... CRAZY FACTS...
STRONGEST STARTING XI... STAR MAN... GAFFER & CAPTAIN...
LAST SEASON IN NUMBERS... MATCH'S VERDICT & MORE!

》INSIDE! 》INSIDE!

32-PAGE MEGA TEAM GUIDE!

- BEST LINE-UPS
- STARS TO WATCH
- BONKERS FACTS
- AWESOME STATS
- MATCH VERDICT
- & LOADS MORE!

15 ELITE PREM POSTERS!

ANDRE GOMES | VARDY | GREENWOOD | MOUNT

PREMIER LEAGUE.. KICK-OFF!

STARS TO WATCH ★ RECORD CHASERS NEW SIGNINGS ★ PREVIEWS & MORE!

FIFA 20 Massive Update PAGE 22

WIN! Ace PlayStation4 Controller! PAGE 13

ADIDAS HARD WIRED BOOTS 》 **FANTASY FOOTY** **MINGS INTERVIEW** 》 **MIEDEMA PROFILE & MORE!**

PACKED EVERY WEEK WITH...

INTERVIEWS & STATS!

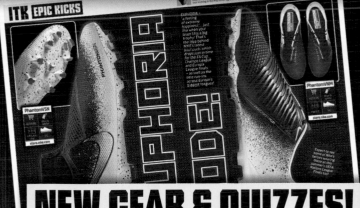

NEW GEAR & QUIZZES!

FIFA TIPS & SKILLS!

BIG STARS & POSTERS!

SUBSCRIBE TO MATCH!...

CALL
01959 543 747
QUOTE: MAT501

ONLINE
SHOP.KELSEY.
CO.UK/MAT501

QUIZ ANSWERS!

Premier League Quiz — Pages 18-19

Flashback: Raul Jimenez.

Aston Villa Quiz: 1. 1874; 2. The Lions; 3. Robert Huth; 4. Second - in 1992-93; 5. True.

Close-Up: 1. Sadio Mane; 2. Heung-min Son; 3. Jamie Vardy; 4. Gylfi Sigurdsson.

Camera Shy: Jonjo Shelvey, James Maddison & James Ward-Prowse.

Stadium Game: 1C; 2D; 3A; 4B.

Freaky Faces: Alexandre Lacazette.

Super Skippers:
Crystal Palace - Luka Milivojevic;
Newcastle - Jamaal Lascelles;
Tottenham - Hugo Lloris;
West Ham - Mark Noble.

Prem Heroes: 1. Bournemouth; 2. Watford; 3. Tottenham; 4. Burnley; 5. Man. United; 6. Leicester; 7. Arsenal; 8. Man. City.

Crazy Kit: Norwich.

Prem Crossword — Page 20

See below.

Internationals Quiz — Pages 34-35

Footy At The Films: Leroy Sane.

Belgium Quiz: 1. The Red Devils; 2. Jan Vertonghen; 3. Romelu Lukaku; 4. True; 5. France.

Close-Up: 1. Neymar; 2. Kylian Mbappe; 3. Gareth Bale; 4. Virgil van Dijk.

Soccer Scrabble: Raheem Sterling.

Spot The Ball: B15.

Name The Country: Salah - Egypt; Pulisic - USA; Silva - Portugal; Taylor - Wales.

Who Am I?: Callum McGregor.

MATCH! Winner: Goncalo Guedes.

Women's World Cup Brain-Buster — Page 36

1. Four; 2. Parc des Princes; 3. Five; 4. Marta; 5. Sweden; 6. USA 2-0 Netherlands; 7. Ettie; 8. Four; 9. Ellen White; 10. Megan Rapinoe.

EFL Quiz — Pages 58-59

On The Box: Jarrod Bowen.

Spot The Ball: F10.

Guess The Winners: 2018-19 - Norwich; 2017-18 - Wolves; 2016-17 - Newcastle; 2015-16 - Burnley.

Footy Mis-Match: See top right.

EFL Wordsearch — Page 60

See below.

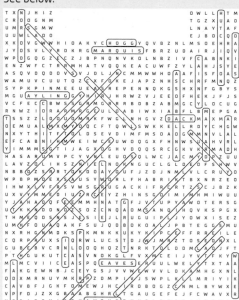

Legends Quiz — Pages 70-71

Game Changer: Steven Gerrard.

The Numbers Game: Four.

Odd One Out: Oliver Kahn.

Trophy Time: Alan Shearer.

One-Club Heroes:
1. Liverpool; 2. Man. United; 3. Arsenal; 4. Southampton; 5. Man. United; 6. Tottenham.

Mega Mash-Up: Ronaldinho.

Action Replay: 1. Portugal; 2. Germany; 3. Zinedine Zidane; 4. Marco Materazzi; 5. Italy 1-1 France; 6. A headbutt; 7. David Trezeguet; 8. Fabio Grosso; 9. True.

Legends Wordfit — Page 72

See below.